on of date

A2 Law

UNIT 5

AQA

Module 5: Law of Tort

Ian Yule & Jennifer Currer

Philip Allan Updates
Market Place
Deddington
Oxfordshire
OX15 0SE

tel: 01869 338652
fax: 01869 337590
e-mail: sales@philipallan.co.uk
www.philipallan.co.uk

© Philip Allan Updates 2006

ISBN-13: 978-1-84489-010-1
ISBN-10: 1-84489-010-4

This guide has been written specifically to support students preparing for the
AQA A2 Law Unit 5 examination. The content has been neither approved nor
endorsed by AQA and remains the sole responsibility of the authors. AQA examination questions are reproduced by permission of the Assessment and
Qualifications Alliance.

Printed by MPG Books, Bodmin

Environmental information
The paper on which this title is printed is sourced from managed, sustainable
forests.

Contents

Introduction

■ ■ ■

Content Guidance

■ ■ ■

Questions and Answers

Introduction

About this guide

The AQA specification for the AS and A2 Law examinations is divided into six modules. Unit 5 covers four separate law options. This guide deals with **Law of Tort** — the most popular option. It builds on the elements of the tort of negligence from Unit 3 and covers nervous shock, pure economic loss, occupiers' liability, nuisance, vicarious liability and *Rylands* v *Fletcher*.

This is a substantive, i.e. 'real law', module, which means that the examination paper will contain problem-solving questions. In order to answer them successfully, candidates must be able to use case law effectively.

The examination for this module is 1 hour 15 minutes. It comprises two questions from which you must select one. Each question consists of three parts. The first two parts are based on a scenario and address the specification topics listed above. The third part is evaluative (as in Unit 4) and requires candidates to consider criticisms of various legal rules developed from cases. This guide includes advice on approaching this part of the unit exam.

There are three sections to this guide:

- **Introduction** — this provides advice on how the guide should be used, an explanation of the skills and terminology required to complete the unit successfully and guidance on revision and examination techniques.
- **Content Guidance** — this sets out the specification content for Unit 5: Law of Tort. It also contains references to cases which you will need to study for a sound understanding of each topic.
- **Questions and Answers** — this section provides sample A- and C-grade answers to typical examination questions on each topic area. The A-grade answers demonstrate how to employ case law and statutory references to best effect. Examiner comments show how marks are awarded or why they are withheld.

How to use this guide

The Content Guidance section covers all the elements for the Unit 5: Law of Tort specification, breaking each topic down into manageable sections for initial study and later revision. It is not intended to be a comprehensive and detailed set of notes for the unit — the material needs to be supplemented by further reading from textbooks and case studies.

When you have finished reading each topic, make a summary of the factual material under the appropriate headings and subheadings of the specification, incorporating additional material from your wider reading and research. Then test yourself by using the sample questions on each topic. By practising questions and assessing your answers against the examiner's comments you will learn how to use your knowledge and understanding to improve your exam grade.

Learning strategies

It is essential to build up a good set of notes for successful A2 study. These notes should be laid out clearly under the headings used in the Content Guidance section, and should contain accurate definitions and explanations, together with relevant case and statutory references. Ideally, you should compile your notes by drawing on a number of sources: this guide, classroom teaching, other textbooks, quality newspapers and legal journals. It is also recommended that you compile summaries of the most important cases for each topic, because most of the rules in this unit are drawn from case law.

Revision planning

At this level of study, it is vital that you understand the need to learn factual information thoroughly. Do this as the module is being taught, topic by topic. Don't leave it until the revision stage, otherwise you will find that there is simply too much detailed information to absorb. Remember that skimming over some notes or reading this guide is *not* revision if you haven't already learned the material.

The first stage of revision requires organisation of all your work. You should ensure that:

- your class notes are up to date
- you have understood the main points of each topic in this guide
- you have made accurate notes on any wider reading
- you have made clear notes about case studies, stating both the key facts and, more importantly, the legal reasoning behind decisions

The next stage is to summarise all of the material, organising it under the headings and subheadings of the Unit 5: Law of Tort specification. During the revision period, you should go though your notes and reduce them to manageable proportions. This is, in itself, an effective learning exercise. The act of summarising makes it easier to recall the material and should reduce the chance of forgetting parts of it in the examination. Most exam marks are not lost through failure to understand the material, but simply through forgetting to include fuller explanations and, in this unit particularly, not using relevant cases.

Assessment objectives

Assessment objectives (AOs) are common to AS and A2 units and are intended to assess a candidate's ability to:

- recall, select, deploy and develop knowledge and understanding of legal principles accurately and by means of examples

- analyse legal material, issues and situations, and evaluate and apply the appropriate legal rules and principles
- present a logical and coherent argument and communicate relevant materials in a clear and effective manner, using correct legal terminology

Examination technique

First of all, familiarise yourself with the style of questions for this unit. Learn from these questions and the AQA mark scheme what the potential content is for each question, and how many marks are allocated across the different mark bands. The last section of this guide — Questions and Answers — is designed to provide guidance about the techniques that are required for this unit.

Case references

The importance of case references cannot be overemphasised. Without them it is impossible to demonstrate a sound understanding of relevant law. A case-free answer rarely obtains more than an E grade, and will more often be awarded a U grade.

Many candidates appear to labour under the misapprehension that as long as some cases are mentioned, it does not matter too much whether or not they are the appropriate ones. Make sure you are able to match cases to the correct legal rule.

While the facts of cases are certainly relevant, especially in Unit 5, the most important aspect of case law is the issue of the legal reasoning employed by senior judges in order to arrive at their decision. Learn to state the basic facts of the case briefly and then go on to explain fully the legal reasons behind the actual case decision. Study the way in which key cases are used in the Questions and Answers section of this guide to demonstrate a fuller understanding of a topic, or to illustrate a key issue or argument.

QWC marks

Ten marks are awarded on each A2 paper for the quality of written communication (QWC). The easiest way to lose some of these marks is to misspell basic legal words such as 'claimant', 'trespasser', 'vicarious', 'negligence' and 'nuisance'. Check your spelling, use paragraphs correctly and make your handwriting as clear as possible.

Planning your answers

When you look at the A-grade answers in the Questions and Answers section of this guide, you will recognise that they have a clear structure, usually demonstrated straight away by a simple, accurate and relevant first sentence. The opening section immediately addresses a key element of the question set, relevant topics are clearly identified with sound explanations provided, and there are many case references that underpin the explanation or argument. Finally, there will be a short paragraph which both summarises the major points of law already explained and provides a clear conclusion. C-grade answers lack this element of planning and structure.

Lack of planning will almost certainly result in at least one grade being lost. In the exam, you have to read two fairly detailed scenarios and then decide which question to attempt. As soon as you have decided which question to answer, make a short but detailed plan for parts (a)–(c) *before* you start to write your answer to part (a). Reread the scenario to ensure that all key issues have been identified, and then consider which are the most important and relevant cases.

Omissions

Leaving out important information is the single greatest cause of losing marks. Spend time reading the question and deciding which legal topics are relevant to the scenario — in many cases, there may be more than one. In this unit, many of the topics overlap, for example negligence rules with nervous shock or pure economic loss, nuisance with *Rylands* v *Fletcher*, or occupiers' liability to both trespassers and lawful visitors.

Time planning

Contrary to popular belief, few students have a problem with lack of time in the examination. By doing homework essays and timed or practice examination essays you will learn whether you are a quick or a slow writer. If you feel that you are likely to have a time problem, planning your response is even more vital. There is no point in wasting time writing material that is either inaccurate or irrelevant. Learn from the A-grade answers in this guide how long your answers should be.

Those who finish early — and this will apply to most candidates — should first check their answers to ensure that they have included key legal rules and appropriate cases. Next they should look at their plans to ensure that they have covered all the relevant points. If at the end of this process there is still time left, they should consider what additional material can be added, such as a further case reference, or a more extensive explanation of a legal rule. Given the narrow grade boundaries which exist in all law papers, even an extra 2 marks could result in a higher grade being achieved.

Content Guidance

The specification for Unit 5: Law of Tort outlined in this section covers the following topics:

Negligence
- Psychiatric injury
- Economic loss
- Negligent misstatement

Occupiers' liability
- The **Occupiers' Liability Act 1957** — the duty owed to lawful visitors
- The **Occupiers' Liability Act 1984** — the duty owed to trespassers

Nuisance
- Private nuisance
- Public nuisance
- Defences
- Ineffectual defences

The rule in *Rylands* v *Fletcher*
- Specific defences

Vicarious liability

General defences
- Contributory negligence
- *Volenti non fit injuria*

Remedies
- Damages
- Injunctions

Negligence

Psychiatric injury

Historically, the law did not extend to claims brought purely in respect of psychiatric injury. The reason cited most often for the denial of such claims was that psychiatric injury is difficult to diagnose. This difficulty of diagnosis leads to the suspicion that victims may fake their symptoms and bring fictitious claims. There is also the fear of 'opening the floodgates' to numerous actions. Nevertheless, in recent years the law of negligence, in particular the scope of the duty of care element, has gradually evolved so that various categories of people may bring a claim, provided that they satisfy the additional specified legal criteria. Once a claimant has satisfied the specific duty of care requirements, the normal rules of breach of duty and causation apply. The three categories of people who can bring an action are:

- primary victims
- secondary victims
- rescuers

A primary victim is someone who suffers psychiatric injury through fear for his or her own safety. A secondary victim is someone who suffers psychiatric injury through fear for another person's safety. A rescuer, as the name suggests, is someone who suffers psychiatric injury as a result of coming to the aid of someone in difficulty.

What is psychiatric injury?

All people who claim for psychiatric injury, whatever category they fall into, must show that they are suffering from a recognised psychiatric illness, capable of resulting from the incident and recognised as having long-term effects. Mere distress, fright, grief and sorrow are insufficient.

Lord Steyn, in *White and Others* v *Chief Constable of South Yorkshire* (1999), recognised the difficulty of distinguishing between two categories of claimants: those who suffer from extreme grief and those whose suffering amounts to a medically recognisable psychiatric illness. While the symptoms could be similar and equally severe, the law only provides redress to the claimants in the second category. The present position of the common law is that conditions such as post-traumatic stress disorder qualify as medically recognisable.

The outcomes of cases concerning this issue are somewhat unpredictable. In *Tredget* v *Bexley Health Authority* (1994), the claimants were held to have suffered psychiatric injury when, due to medical negligence, their child was born with serious injuries and died 2 days later. It was argued that they had suffered no more than profound grief. The decision of the Court of Appeal in *Vernon* v *Bosley* (1997) to hold that pathological grief disorder was medically recognisable, blurred the distinction further.

Primary victims

A primary victim is a person who suffers psychiatric injury as a result of being directly affected by the negligent act, or who fears for his/her own safety. The early case law on psychiatric injury established that a person could claim if he/she was within the range of potential physical injury. In *Dulieu* v *White and Sons* (1901), the claimant suffered psychiatric injury when a horse-drawn van was driven into the public house where she was working. Kennedy LJ remarked that it was not necessary to suffer physical harm through impact. It was sufficient that the psychiatric injury was caused through a 'reasonable fear of immediate personal injury to oneself'.

The distinction between primary and secondary victims was considered in some depth by the House of Lords in *Page* v *Smith* (1995). The claimant was in a car accident caused by the negligent driving of the defendant. He was not physically injured but the incident sparked a recurrence of his illness known as ME. He claimed that this recurrence had been caused by the shock of being in the accident. The defendant was held liable. Two important distinctions between primary and secondary victims were emphasised by the House of Lords. First, it stated that the primary victim does not need to show that psychiatric injury was foreseeable, merely that some kind of personal injury was foreseeable. Once this is established, it is irrelevant whether the primary victim suffers physical harm as well as psychiatric harm. Second, on the issue of the recurrence of a condition to which the claimant was predisposed, the Lords said that the primary victim does not need to be a person of normal fortitude. Lord Lloyd commented that a claimant for physical injury does not need to satisfy such a requirement and said: 'There is no difference in principle between an egg-shell skull and an egg-shell personality.' The 'egg-shell personality' rule applies to claims for psychiatric injury; therefore, the defendant must take the primary victim as he/she finds them.

Conclusion on primary victims

A successful primary victim will need to prove that:

- he/she is suffering from a medically recognised psychiatric illness
- personal injury, physical and/or psychiatric, was foreseeable

Secondary victims

A secondary victim suffers psychiatric injury not as a result of being directly involved in the event or fearing for his or her own safety, but as a result of fearing for someone else's safety. More stringent criteria apply to secondary victims than to primary victims, not least because of the potentially endless liability that could attach to the defendant.

The law of negligence has long recognised the duty owed to secondary victims. In *Hambrook* v *Stokes Bros* (1925), the successful claimant suffered nervous shock when she witnessed a driverless lorry careering down a narrow street in the direction of her children. Bankes LJ used as illustration a hypothetical situation in which a lorry was heading towards two mothers, each holding a baby. One suffered shock through fear for her own safety and the other suffered shock through fear for her baby's safety. He questioned whether the law only allowed a claim in respect of the mother fearing for her own safety and concluded that both mothers would be able to claim. However, the Court of Appeal did stipulate that the secondary victim must perceive the event with his or her own sight or hearing. The law does not compensate for psychiatric injury brought about through communication by a third party.

The 'control mechanisms' applicable to secondary victims, which the Court of Appeal had begun to set out in *Hambrook*, were explored thoroughly by the House of Lords in *Alcock* v *Chief Constable of South Yorkshire* (1991). This case concerned numerous claims made by relatives and friends of the 95 people killed and the 400 people injured when the police negligently allowed an excessive number of people into the Hillsborough football ground. The Law Lords were in agreement that:
- there must be close ties of love and affection
- the psychiatric injury must be caused through the victim's own sight and hearing or the immediate aftermath
- the injury must be caused by the sudden appreciation of a horrifying event

Close ties of love and affection
The requirement that the secondary victim has close ties of love and affection with the primary victim is to be presumed between spouses and between parents and children. However, the Law Lords emphasised that close ties could exist in other kinds of family relationships and in close friendships. Lord Keith commented that close ties may sometimes be stronger in the case of engaged couples than in the case of couples who have been married for years. Close ties in these relationships (other than spouses or parent and child) must be proved by the claimant and are decided on a case-by-case basis.

Psychiatric injury must be caused through the victim's own sight and hearing or the immediate aftermath
There are two aspects to this control mechanism. The claimant must:
- perceive the event with his or her own unaided senses, or
- witness the immediate aftermath of the event

The claimant must perceive the event with his or her own unaided senses
The psychiatric injury must be caused by the claimant's sight or hearing of the event. It is not sufficient to read about it or learn about it through a third party.

In *Alcock*, many of the claimants had watched the disaster unfold on television. The issue of whether simultaneous broadcasting of a disaster could be regarded as equivalent to seeing or hearing the event was left open. The Lords did not have to clarify the position on this because the television companies had conformed to the television authority's code of ethics and had not shown the suffering of any recognisable individual. Consequently, the Lords were in agreement that the pictures televised could not be equated with seeing or hearing the event or witnessing its immediate aftermath.

However, the Lords did consider that there may be circumstances in which viewing simultaneous broadcasts could be equivalent to seeing or hearing the event.

The claimant must witness the immediate aftermath of the event
The Lords agreed unanimously in *Alcock* that the psychiatric injury could be caused through witnessing the immediate aftermath of the accident.

The extension of the law of negligence to those who suffer psychiatric injury as a result of witnessing the immediate aftermath of an accident was settled by Lord Wilberforce in *McLoughlin* v *O'Brian* (1982). The claimant was told that her family had been involved in an accident. She arrived at the hospital, approximately 2 hours after the accident had occurred, where she saw her husband and two of her three children injured and covered in mud and oil. She learned from her husband that their other child had been killed. The other Law Lords agreed with Lord Wilberforce that the law should be extended to cover the immediate aftermath, as this was what justice demanded. As Lord Wilberforce had pointed out, there was little difference between this case and cases where claims had been allowed before. For example, in *Benson* v *Lee* (1972), the successful claimant, a mother in her home 100 yards away from the accident, was told by a third party that her children had been injured; the women then suffered shock upon running out and witnessing the accident scene.

While it remains unclear as to precisely what amounts to the immediate aftermath in terms of time span, it appears that the victims must be in their immediate post-accident state and not, for example, cleaned up. In *Jaensch* v *Coffey* (1984), the claimant saw her husband at the hospital before and between emergency operations. Deane J in the Australian High Court said:

> The aftermath of the accident extended to the hospital to which the injured person was taken and persisted for so long as he remained in the state produced by the accident up to and including immediate post-accident treatment.

In *Alcock*, the House of Lords overruled earlier cases, including *Hevican* v *Ruane* (1991), which had held that the immediate aftermath extended to witnessing a body in the mortuary.

The psychiatric injury must be caused suddenly
The psychiatric injury must be induced by shock. Lord Ackner explained this in terms of 'the sudden appreciation by sight or sound of a horrifying event, which violently agitates the mind'. Psychiatric injury caused gradually over a period of time is not recoverable.

In *Jaensch* v *Coffey*, Brennan J commented that those suffering psychiatric injury caused by looking after an injured spouse, or by the wayward conduct of a brain-damaged child, would have no claim.

The injustice of the sudden shock requirement is illustrated by the case of *Sion* v *Hampstead Health Authority* (1994). A father suffered psychiatric injury as a result of watching his son die over a period of 14 days. His claim was unsuccessful as the psychiatric injury was not induced by shock.

Psychiatric injury must be foreseeable
While primary victims only need to prove that personal injury, be it physical and/or psychiatric, was foreseeable, secondary victims must prove that psychiatric injury was foreseeable. In *Page* v *Smith*, Lord Lloyd of Berwick distinguished between primary and secondary victims. He said: 'In claims by secondary victims...the defendant will not be liable unless psychiatric injury is foreseeable in a person of normal fortitude. These control mechanisms have no place where the claimant is the primary victim.'

The secondary victim must be a person of normal fortitude
It is clear from the words of Lord Lloyd of Berwick cited above, that had the claimant in *Page* v *Smith* been a secondary victim, his claim would have been unsuccessful due to his predisposition to ME. Claims by secondary victims will only be successful if the secondary victim is a person of normal fortitude.

Conclusion on secondary victims
A successful secondary victim will need to show that:
- he/she is suffering from a medically recognised psychiatric illness
- he/she has close ties of love and affection with the primary victim
- the injury was caused through his/her own sight or hearing or the immediate aftermath
- the psychiatric illness was caused suddenly
- psychiatric injury was foreseeable
- he/she is a person of normal fortitude

Rescuers

The law recognises that danger invites rescue. Tort-feasors are thus expected to be liable to those who try to save their victims. As Stuart-Smith LJ commented in *McFarlane* v *EE Caledonia Ltd* (1994): 'A tort-feasor who has put A in peril by his negligence must reasonably foresee that B may come to rescue him, even if it involves risking his own safety.'

In *Chadwick* v *British Transport Commission* (1967), the claimant suffered anxiety neurosis as a result of helping at the scene of a serious railway crash in which 90 people were killed. He was asked, because of his small size, to crawl into the carriages to help the injured. The claim was successful. Danger and injury to passengers was foreseeable, as was danger and injury to someone who tried to rescue them. Similarly, in *Hale* v *London Underground* (1992), the claimant, who was a fireman involved in rescuing people from the fire in King's Cross underground station, was able to recover damages for the post-traumatic stress disorder caused to him by the event.

The question as to who qualifies as a rescuer was closely examined by the House of Lords in *White* v *Chief Constable of South Yorkshire Police* (1999). The claimants were police officers, who suffered post-traumatic stress disorder as a result of helping to deal with the consequences of the Hillsborough tragedy. The Court of Appeal held that three of the police officers qualified as rescuers because they gave assistance in the immediate aftermath of the disaster. The House of Lords reversed the Court of Appeal decision. Lord Steyn said that, in order to recover compensation for psychiatric injury, a rescuer must satisfy the requirement that he/she objectively placed him or herself in danger, or reasonably perceived him or herself as doing so. None of the claimants were exposed to danger at any time and neither did they believe that they were so exposed. Therefore, they were not considered rescuers.

The decision in *White* v *Chief Constable of South Yorkshire Police* has since been criticised as limiting liability towards rescuers. However, Lord Steyn specifically referred to *Chadwick* as being an example of the claimant placing himself in danger: 'There was clearly a danger the carriage might collapse.' He also cited Waller J who, in deciding the 1967 case, had referred to the 'element of personal danger in what Mr Chadwick was doing'. Many key cases would appear to support the view of Lord Steyn. In *Hale* v *London Underground*, the fireman placed himself in danger by going into the underground station, and in *Haynes* v *Harwood* (1935), the claimant police constable placed himself in danger by trying to stop a runaway horse.

Rescuers who are not able to prove the 'placed themselves in danger' criterion have the option to claim as secondary victims, the success of which will depend on whether they are able to satisfy the control mechanisms.

Conclusion on rescuers

A successful rescuer will have to prove that:
- he/she is suffering from a medically recognised psychiatric illness
- he/she placed himself/herself in danger or perceived that he/she was in danger

Bystanders

The law of negligence does not allow bystanders to recover for psychiatric injury. As Lord Wilberforce explained in *McLoughlin* v *O'Brian*, the law denies claims of the ordinary bystander because 'such persons must be assumed to be possessed of fortitude sufficient to enable them to endure the calamities of modern life', and because 'defendants cannot be expected to compensate the world at large'.

In *Bourhill* v *Young* (1943), a woman claimed damages for nervous shock caused by an accident that happened 45–50 feet from where she was standing, between the defendant motorcyclist and a car. She did not see the collision but did hear the sound of it, and later saw blood on the road. She admitted that she did not fear immediate bodily injury to herself. Her appeal was dismissed on the basis that the defendant could not have anticipated that the claimant would be affected by his actions and, therefore, did not owe her a duty of care. Lord Porter said: 'The appellant was never herself in any bodily danger nor reasonably in fear of danger either for herself or others.' The appellant in *Bourhill* did not qualify as a primary victim, a secondary victim or a rescuer. Accordingly, her claim failed, on the basis that she was a bystander.

The possibility of bystanders being able to successfully claim has not, however, been completely ruled out. In *Alcock*, Lord Keith said: 'The case of a bystander unconnected with the victims of an accident is difficult. Psychiatric injury to him would not ordinarily, in my view, be within the range of reasonable foreseeability, but could not perhaps be entirely excluded from it if the circumstances of a catastrophe occurring very close to him were particularly horrific.'

While the judiciary have allowed for the possibility of bystanders bringing claims in the future, the courts have nevertheless been reluctant to extend the law in this way. In *McFarlane* v *EE Caledonia Ltd* (1994), the claimant was on a support vessel some 100 metres from the oilrig on which he normally worked, when the oilrig caught fire. He helped prepare the heli-hanger to receive casualties by moving blankets, and assisted two of the walking wounded as they arrived on the support vessel. The claimant relied on the dicta of Lord Keith in *Alcock*, expressing the view that it was difficult to imagine a more horrific disaster than the holocaust on the oilrig, especially as he knew his workmates were on board. The Court of Appeal held that he could not recover damages. Stuart-Smith LJ said:

> The court should not extend the duty to those who are mere bystanders or witnesses of horrific events unless there is a sufficient degree of proximity, which requires both nearness in time and place and a close relationship of love and affection between claimant and victim.

The Court of Appeal did not adopt the dicta of Lord Keith, preferring instead to keep the categories of eligible claimant to primary victims, secondary victims and rescuers.

Conclusion on bystanders

Bystanders do not qualify either as primary victims, secondary victims or rescuers. They are unable to recover compensation for the psychiatric injury they are caused.

An evaluation of psychiatric injury

In *White* v *Chief Constable of South Yorkshire* (1999), Lord Steyn commented: 'The law on the recovery of compensation for pure psychiatric harm is a patchwork quilt of distinctions which are difficult to justify.' Lord Steyn recognises that the mechanisms developed by the judiciary, in order to prevent the number of potential claims in respect of psychiatric injury, result in injustice.

Injustice caused by the requirement that the psychiatric injury be medically recognised

The courts have always shown reluctance in allowing claims for psychiatric injury. Until the twentieth century the position was, as stated by the Privy Council in *Victorian Railways Comrs* v *Coultas* (1888), that compensation for psychiatric injury was not recoverable at all. The reason given by the Privy Council for denying the claim was that little was known about the workings of the mind. As science has advanced, the courts have become more willing to allow psychiatric injury claims. However, as Lord Hoffman commented in *White v Chief Constable of South Yorkshire Police*: 'Despite scientific advances, this remains a serious problem.'

The courts allow a claimant to recover damages only when his/her condition amounts to a recognised psychiatric illness. Conditions such as fear, anxiety or grief are considered to be normal consequences of a distressing event and not deserving of compensation. The problems with this are twofold:

1 Difficulty in defining what amounts to medically recognised psychiatric injury

It is unclear what will amount to a recognised psychiatric illness. While it is clear that conditions such as post-traumatic stress disorder are recoverable, the law is less clear about conditions that may be argued amount to no more than profound grief. In *Vernon v Bosley* (1997), the Court of Appeal allowed a claim by a father who had witnessed the unsuccessful attempt to rescue his children from a car, which had crashed into a river. The Court of Appeal made a fine distinction in this case between ordinary grief and bereavement — which remain irrecoverable — and pathological grief disorder — which was the recognised illness suffered by the father.

2 Grief and anxiety may be just as severe as medically recognised psychiatric injury

The suffering sustained by a person through grief or anxiety may be just as devastating as the suffering sustained through a recognised psychiatric illness or the 'pain and suffering' consequent upon physical harm, yet compensation will only be awarded in respect of the latter types of injury.

Problems caused by the close-ties mechanism

Why presume close ties in respect of spouses, and parents and children?

Close ties of love and affection are presumed between spouses and between parents and children. In other relationships the close ties have to be specifically proved. While it is a positive development to recognise that all manner of relationships could potentially be close, it is not always correct to presume that a relationship between a married couple or between a parent and child is a close one. Lord Keith in *Alcock* commented that close ties may be stronger in the case of engaged couples than between husbands and wives.

Extra burden placed on those who have to prove their close ties

The requirement to prove close ties with the primary victim inevitably makes the court hearing more traumatic for the claimant. It is questionable whether subjecting the personal lives and relationships of claimants to detailed scrutiny can be justified, at a time when, if their claims are true, they are emotionally weak and vulnerable.

Is the close-ties mechanism necessary?

It can be argued that the requirement to prove close ties is unnecessary, as all claimants have to prove they are suffering from a recognised psychiatric illness. The point here is that it is unlikely that a person would suffer such illness if he/she did not have close ties with the primary victim. People are rarely psychologically affected by what happens to those they dislike or those with whom they have little or no contact.

How does the close-ties mechanism relate to witnessing property being destroyed?

The Court of Appeal, in *Attia* v *British Gas* (1988), allowed the claimant to recover compensation for psychiatric injury caused by witnessing the defendant negligently damaging her property. This decision is difficult to reconcile with decisions that have denied the claims of secondary victims such as those in *Alcock* who witnessed the suffering of relatives.

Why is there an unaided senses requirement?

In *Alcock* the Law Lords emphasised the need for the secondary victim to have perceived the event with his/her own unaided senses. Claims by relatives and friends who had watched the disaster on television were rejected. The conclusion of Lord Wilberforce in *McLoughlin* v *O'Brian* that the psychiatric injury must be caused through sight or hearing of the event or its immediate aftermath was upheld.

It is possible that this requirement results in the rejection of some claims that are more deserving than those that are upheld. The impact on a person who hears an event transmitted via a radio, television or mobile telephone could be just as great, or greater, than it would have been through actual sight or hearing. The experience may be all the more traumatic because of the helplessness experienced at not being able to go to the aid of the victim. The potential injustice of this control mechanism was highlighted in *Boylan* v *Keegan* (2001). An 8-year-old girl was badly injured in a road accident. Her mother who was present at the scene telephoned the father who heard the girl's screams and the ambulance sirens. The girl died in her father's arms 2 days later. The court rejected the father's claim in respect of the psychiatric injury caused by the accident, as he had not perceived the event with his own unaided senses and had not been present at the immediate aftermath.

Uncertainty regarding the scope of the immediate aftermath

In *Jaensch* v *Coffey*, an Australian case, the claimant was successful in recovering damages for psychiatric injury sustained as a result of seeing her injured husband at the hospital before he underwent a series of emergency operations. Deane J said:

> The aftermath of the accident extended to the hospital to which the injured person was taken and persisted for so long as he remained in the state produced by the accident up to and including immediate post-accident treatment.

Lord Wilberforce followed the approach of Deane J in *McLoughlin* v *O'Brian*. The claimant was informed that her husband and children had been involved in an accident. She arrived at the hospital approximately 2 hours after the accident had occurred to find her family still covered with oil and mud, and distraught with pain, and was informed that her daughter had died. Lord Wilberforce commented that this was at the margin of what the courts would allow to constitute the immediate aftermath. The outcome of these two cases is that the person who arrives at the hospital before his or her relatives have been attended to by medical staff will recover compensation for psychiatric injury caused, but the person who arrives after treatment has started will not. Professor Michael A. Jones in *Liability for Psychiatric Illness — More Principle, Less Subtlety*, comments: 'Liability for psychiatric illness should not depend upon a race between the claimant and the ambulance.'

In *Alcock,* the Law Lords refused to extend the scope of the immediate aftermath to identifying a body at a mortuary some 8 hours or more after the event. Lord Ackner said that while the identification could be described as part of the aftermath, it could not be described as part of the immediate aftermath. He pointed out that Lord Wilberforce had commented that the facts in *McLoughlin* v *O'Brian* were on the margin of what the law would allow. The Law Lords doubted that the decision reached in *Hevican* v *Ruane,* in which a father had successfully claimed in respect of identifying his son's body at the mortuary 3 hours after the death, was correct.

From these cases it can be concluded that the immediate aftermath extends to a time limit of somewhere less than 8 hours after the event but probably nearer to 2 hours. It would appear unlikely that identification of a body will fall within the immediate aftermath. Primary victims must be in the same state they would have been in at the time of the accident if the secondary victim is to make a successful claim. However, the judiciary has so far not taken the step of defining the scope of the immediate aftermath, leaving the outcomes of future cases somewhat unpredictable on this issue.

Injustice caused by the sudden shock mechanism

Lord Ackner in *Alcock* said:

> 'Shock' in the context of this cause of action, involves the sudden appreciation by sight or sound of a horrifying event, which violently agitates the mind. It has yet to include psychiatric illness caused by the accumulation over a period of time of more gradual assaults on the nervous system.

The injustice of this requirement is illustrated by the facts of *Sion* v *Hampstead Health Authority.* A father suffered psychiatric injury as a result of watching his son die over a period of 14 days. His claim was unsuccessful, as his psychiatric illness was not induced by shock.

The judiciary have nevertheless shown willingness to mitigate the injustice of the sudden shock requirement by extending it to cover some lengthy events. In *Tredget* v *Bexley Health Authority*, a baby was born with serious injuries, from which it died 2 days later. The parents were successful in their claim. The defendants argued, unsuccessfully, that the parents' psychiatric illness was not caused suddenly but rather through a gradual realisation of events. Similarly, in *Walters* v *North Glamorgan NHST* a 10-month-old baby was taken to hospital suffering from jaundice, and the hospital negligently underestimated the seriousness of his condition. Very early next morning, the baby's mother (who was sleeping in the same room at the hospital) woke to find the baby having a fit. Doctors assured her that the baby would recover, and it was sent to a London hospital by ambulance, where on arrival it was found to have suffered irreversible brain damage. The following day, the baby's parents agreed that life support should be withdrawn, and the baby died in its mother's arms. The mother suffered a 'pathological grief reaction', and the judge awarded damages on the basis of a 36-hour-long 'shocking event'.

Disagreement as to who should qualify as a rescuer

The case of *White* v *Chief Constable of South Yorkshire Police* (1999) is significant because the House of Lords appeared to restrict the number of people who may qualify as rescuers. The majority Law Lords held that rescuers are people who objectively place themselves in danger or reasonably believe they are doing so. The Lords justified their decision by reference to comments made by both the judge and counsel in *Chadwick* v *British Transport Commission*. Two judges, Lord Goff and Lord Griffiths, dissented.

In *Chadwick*, the claimant had helped with the rescue operation following a train crash. He entered a wrecked train carriage to help the injured. Lord Steyn cited Waller J, the judge at first instance, who said: 'Although there was clearly an element of personal danger in what Mr Chadwick was doing, I think I must deal with this case on the basis that it was the horror of the whole experience which caused his reaction.' Lord Hoffman, another majority judge, referred to the comments of Lord Griffiths who, as the successful counsel for Mr Chadwick had argued: 'Mr Chadwick might have been injured by a wrecked carriage collapsing on him as he worked among the injured. A duty of care is owed to a rescuer in such circumstances.' Thus, the majority judges were able to argue that their decision was based on a principle long established by the courts.

Lord Goff rejected the argument that *Chadwick* had been decided on the basis of Mr Chadwick having placed himself in danger. He pointed out that Waller J expressly stated that he was dealing with the case 'on the basis that it was the horror of the whole experience which caused his reaction'. Lord Goff also pointed out the injustice that could result from the decision of the majority judges. He used as illustration the example of two rescuers entering a train to help the injured. Helping at the front of the train involved exposure to danger but helping at the back did not. If the service provided by both helpers was the same and the effect on the psychiatric health of both rescuers was the same, what was the justification for allowing one to recover damages and not the other?

It is questionable whether bystanders should be barred from making a claim

The case law would appear for the present to have established that bystanders cannot recover damages for psychiatric injury. However, the judiciary is not totally in agreement that the door should remain closed to such claims. In *Alcock*, Lord Keith said *in obiter*:

> The case of a bystander unconnected with the victims of an accident is difficult. Psychiatric injury to him would not ordinarily, in my view, be within the range of reasonable foreseeability, but could not perhaps be entirely excluded from it if the circumstances of a catastrophe occurring very close to him were particularly horrific.

Lord Ackner, with whom Lord Oliver specifically agreed on this issue, made similar comments. Using the example of a petrol tanker careering out of control into a school and bursting into flames, he said: 'I would not be prepared to rule out a potential claim by a passer-by so shocked by the scene as to suffer psychiatric illness.'

Subsequent to these comments in *Alcock*, both the Court of Appeal in *McFarlane* v *EE Caledonia Ltd*, and the House of Lords in *White* v *Chief Constable of South Yorkshire Police*, seemingly closed the door to claims from bystanders. In both of these cases, the decisions were acknowledged by the judiciary to cause hardship to the claimants concerned but were justified on policy grounds.

In *McFarlane*, the claimant, a worker on the Piper Alpha oilrig, which caught fire, witnessed the disaster from a support vessel situated approximately 100 metres from the oilrig. He helped receive casualties onto the support vessel but was unable to recover damages for the psychiatric injury caused to him by the event. Stuart LJ acknowledged the comments of Lord Keith in *Alcock* but held that, 'as a matter of principle and policy', those who were mere bystanders or witnesses of horrific events must satisfy the control mechanisms applicable to secondary victims.

In *White*, the House of Lords held that a claim brought by police officers on duty at the Hillsborough football stadium should fail. The officers were not primary victims or rescuers, as they had not placed themselves in danger or perceived themselves as doing so. They could not satisfy the requirements of the control mechanisms applicable to secondary victims. Lord Steyn acknowledged that the police officers had suffered debilitating psychiatric harm and said that their claims for compensation could not be lightly dismissed. However, he said: 'It is settled law that bystanders at tragic events, even if they suffer foreseeable psychiatric harm, are not entitled to recover damages.' In justifying the House of Lords decision Lord Steyn made reference to policy issues, including the need to limit the liability of the defendant, the fear of opening the floodgates and the danger of fraudulent claims, and the potential injustice of allowing police officers, but not the relatives of the dead and injured, to recover damages.

The decisions in *McFarlane* and *White* were clearly based on policy considerations rather than on what would be a just outcome for the claimants.

Justification for control mechanisms

Throughout the case law concerned with psychiatric injury claims, the judiciary is at pains to explain that there are policy reasons for restricting the number of claimants. These policy reasons may be summarised as the need to:

- avoid opening the floodgates making courts unable to deal with the sheer volume of claims
- avoid fraudulent claims (made possible due to the continuing difficulty of diagnosis)
- limit the potential liability of the defendant to a level that is acceptable, especially to insurance companies

Reform

The Law Commission has recognised many of the issues raised above. The key recommendations in its Report of 1998 may be summarised as follows:

- The requirement that psychiatric illness be induced by shock should no longer apply.
- The requirement of closeness (in time and space) to the accident or its aftermath, in respect of those who suffer psychiatric injury as a result of harm being caused to those with whom the claimant has close ties, should no longer apply.
- The categories of people who should be deemed to have close ties of love and affection would be the immediate victim's spouse, either parent of the immediate victim, any child of the immediate victim, any brother or sister of the immediate victim and the immediate victim's cohabitant.

While the Law Commission's recommendations go some way to addressing the problems with the law on psychiatric injury, it has decided that legislative reform is not necessary for many problematic issues including the position of rescuers and bystanders.

Conclusion

There can be little doubt that the law relating to psychiatric injury has been developed with policy, rather than justice for the victims, in mind. As Lord Steyn commented in *White* v *Chief Constable of South Yorkshire Police*:

> In an ideal world, all those who have suffered as a result of the negligence ought to be compensated. But we do not live in Utopia: we live in a practical world where the tort system imposes limits to the classes of claims that rank for consideration as well as to the heads of recoverable damages. This results, of course, in imperfect justice but it is by and large the best that the common law can do.

Economic loss

The law of tort does not generally allow recovery of compensation for pure economic loss. However, similarly to the law relating to psychiatric injury, the rules concerning when a duty of care is owed have been adapted by the courts. In limited circumstances, a claim for economic loss suffered as a result of the defendant's negligence may be made when the economic loss:

- is the direct result of damage to property or personal injury (consequential economic loss)
- is caused by a negligent misstatement
- arises from circumstances the courts have held to fall within the extended Hedley Byrne principle

As with questions that raise issues of psychiatric injury, students should remember that economic loss is a special duty situation within the law of negligence. A claimant will therefore have to prove not only that the defendant owed a duty of care, but also that there was a breach of duty that caused the claimant's loss.

Consequential economic loss

The position, as clarified by Lord Denning in *Spartan Steel and Alloys Ltd* v *Martin and Co Ltd* (1973), is that economic loss, which is consequent upon physical damage or injury, is recoverable in negligence, but there is no liability in respect of pure economic loss arising from negligent acts. In this case, the defendants negligently severed an electricity cable supplying power to the claimants' factory. As a result, the factory had to shut down. The claimants claimed compensation for:

- damage to goods in production at the time of the power cut, i.e. physical damage
- loss of profit on the damaged goods, i.e. consequential economic loss
- loss of profit on goods which could not be manufactured due to the power cut, i.e. pure economic loss

The Court of Appeal held by a majority that compensation could be recovered for the damage to goods in production at the time of the power cut and the loss of profit that would have been made on those goods. The loss of profit that would have been made on the goods in production at the time of the power cut was clearly a consequence of the physical damage to the goods. However, no damage had been caused in respect of the goods that would have been manufactured later that same day. The loss of profit in respect of those goods was thus purely economic and was therefore not recoverable. In so deciding, the Court of Appeal followed the long-established approach taken by the courts.

In *Weller and Co* v *Foot and Mouth Disease Research Institute* (1966), an auctioneer's regular income from the sale of cattle was disrupted as the result of a ban on the movement of livestock following the escape of a virus from the defendants' laboratory. No liability could be imposed for the auctioneer's loss of profit. No damage to property or personal injury was suffered by the auctioneer and his loss was thus purely economic.

More recent decisions illustrate that the courts are anxious to retain the principle that pure economic loss is irrecoverable, even in circumstances where this results in a harsh decision for the claimant. In *Merlin* v *British Nuclear Fuels* (1990), the claimants found radioactive dust in their house. In order to safeguard the health of themselves and their children, they attempted to sell the house and move, but were unable to do so due to the diminution in price caused by the presence of the dust. Despite the increased risk of developing cancer, their claim was unsuccessful. There was no damage to the property and the loss sustained by the claimants was purely economic.

The justification for pure economic loss not being recoverable is one of policy. Clearly, all three types of loss suffered by the claimants in *Spartan Steel* were foreseeable and according to the law of negligence alone should have been recoverable. The courts are cautious about allowing compensation claims in respect of pure economic loss due to the desire to limit the potential liability of defendants to a reasonable level. In *Spartan Steel* Lord Denning MR stated:

> At bottom I think the question of recovering economic loss is one of policy. Whenever the courts draw a line to mark out the bounds of duty, they do it as a matter of policy so as to limit the responsibility of the defendant.

The same policy reasons were behind the decision in *Weller*. In that case, Widgery J explained that the duty owed was only to cattle owners who suffered physical damage due to their cattle being destroyed. Foreseeability alone was insufficient to determine liability, because while the loss caused to the auctioneer was foreseeable, so too was loss to other traders who would normally have enjoyed an increase in business on auction day due to the influx of visitors to the area. To have allowed all these people to claim damages would have increased the liability of the defendants to an unreasonable level.

Compensation in respect of defective products is not recoverable in negligence. It is considered that liability in these instances may only be imposed through the law of contract. There was some doubt about the relationship between negligence and contract following the decision of the House of Lords in *Junior Books Ltd* v *Veitchi Co Ltd* (1983), in which a claim for compensation was allowed in respect of a defectively laid floor.

However, subsequent judgements appear to have confined the decision to the facts in that case.

In *D and F Estates Ltd* v *Church Commissioners for England* (1988), the claimants brought an action against the defendant builders in respect of negligent plasterwork that had become loose and needed replacing. The claim was unsuccessful as the cost of repairing the defective plaster was pure economic loss. The loose plaster had caused neither damage to property nor personal injury.

Murphy v *Brentwood* (1990) clarified the position regarding buildings and defective foundations. The claimant bought a property constructed on a concrete raft on an in-filled site. The raft foundation, which had been approved by the council, was defective and caused serious cracks to appear in the house. Unable to afford the cost of repairing the property to make it safe and habitable, estimated at £45,000, the claimant sold the house at a loss of £35,000. The defendant council was not held liable for the loss. The court held that foundations of a building could not be treated as separate from the building. The building was therefore defective and the cost of repairing the building was purely economic. The House of Lords departed from the decision in *Anns* v *Merton London Borough Council* (1978), where on similar facts a local authority had been held liable in respect of negligently approving inadequate foundations.

Negligent misstatement

Traditionally, the claimant who suffered economic loss caused by statements would have had to bring an action in the tort of deceit. The law as it stands today developed from the dissenting judgement of Lord Denning in *Candler* v *Crane Christmas and Co* (1951). In this case, the defendants negligently prepared a company's accounts. The defendants were aware that the accounts were to be shown to the claimant in order to induce him to invest in the company. The claimant lost money he had subsequently invested, but the court held that the defendants were not liable. Lord Denning dissenting said the defendants owed a duty of care to their 'employer or client, and...any third person to whom they themselves show the accounts, or to whom they know their employer is going to show the accounts so as to induce them to invest money or take some other action on them'.

Lord Denning's dissenting judgement was accepted by the House of Lords, in *obiter*, in *Hedley Byrne and Co Ltd* v *Heller and Partners* (1964). A company called Easipower asked an advertising company to run a campaign. The advertising company approached Easipower's bank for a credit reference. The bank gave a satisfactory reference without checking Easipower's current financial standing. This included a disclaimer. Easipower went into liquidation and the advertising company lost over £17,000. The House of Lords held that liability for economic loss arising from a negligent misstatement could arise in such circumstances but that in this particular case the bank was not liable because of the disclaimer.

The existence of a special relationship

The House of Lords held that in addition to the requirements of foreseeability, proximity and it being fair, just and reasonable to impose a duty, there must be a special relationship between the parties for a duty of care to give careful advice to arise. However, the Law Lords all gave differing accounts of what amounts to a special relationship. Lord Reid said that a special relationship arises:

> ...where it is plain that the party seeking information or advice was trusting the other to exercise such a degree of care as the circumstances required, where it was reasonable for him to do that, and where the other gave the information or advice when he knew or ought to have known that the inquirer was relying on him. I say 'ought to have known' because in questions of negligence we now apply the objective standard of what the reasonable man would have done.

Lord Morris emphasised the importance of the defendant being possessed of a special skill that he exercises to assist another and then stated:

> If, in a sphere in which a person is so placed that others could reasonably rely on his judgement or his skill or on his ability to make careful inquiry, a person takes it on himself to give information or advice to, or allows his information or advice to be passed on to, another person who, as he knows or should know, will place reliance on it, then a duty of care will arise.

Lord Devlin said that he was happy to adopt any of the other Law Lords' statements and also expressed his respect for the statement by Denning LJ in *Candler* v *Crane* about the circumstances in which a duty to take care in making a statement exists. However, in his judgement, Lord Devlin did state that the duty to use care when making a statement arises when there is 'an assumption of responsibility in circumstances in which, but for the absence of consideration, there would be a contract'.

While these statements vary in terms of emphasis, it would appear that a special relationship has the three requirements outlined below.

1 The defendant must possess special skill

In *Mutual Life and Citizens Assurance Co* v *Evatt* (1971), the Privy Council held that an insurance company did not owe a duty of care in giving investment advice. A duty only arose when the defendant was in the business of giving that type of advice, or had professed to have special skill or knowledge in the field in which the advice was given.

The defendant will thus not be liable for statements made informally or in a social situation. A case which seemingly provides an exception to this is *Chaudhry* v *Prabhakar* (1988), in which the claimant had asked a friend to find a suitable car for her. The friend recommended a car that was later discovered to have been in an accident. The decision to hold the defendant liable was justified on the basis that he should have been as careful about giving advice as he would have been if he had been buying the car for himself.

2 The claimant must rely on the statement to his/her detriment

There must be actual reliance and consequent detriment suffered. In *JEB Fastener Ltd v Marks Bloom and Co* (1983), a negligent statement was made about the value of a company's stock. The claimant did not succeed in his claim as he had not relied on this advice. He had bought the company in order to secure the services of the directors, and thus placed no reliance on the value of the stock.

The reliance element of a special relationship has been important in determining the liability of surveyors in giving house valuations. In *Yianni* v *Evans* (1981), the claimants were purchasers of a property bought with the aid of a mortgage from a building society. The defendants were instructed by the building society to value the property in order to establish that it was worth the value of the mortgage. The defendants' valuation stated that the property was suitable as security for a loan of £12,000. The claimants did not have their own survey carried out but relied on the favourable report of the defendants. They purchased the property and then discovered that it needed £18,000 worth of repairs. The High Court held that the defendants were liable. Park J said the defendants knew that the part of the report that confirmed the property was sufficiently valuable to be security for the loan would be passed to the claimants:

> I am sure that the defendants knew that their valuation would be passed on to the claimants and that the defendants knew that the claimants would rely on it when they decided to accept the building society's offer.

Park J referred to the evidence that 90% of applicants for building society mortgages over the previous 6 years had relied on building society surveys. Also important was the fact that the house was at the lower value end of the property market. Accordingly, the purchasers would have been of modest means and therefore would not be expected to obtain an independent valuation.

This decision was approved by the House of Lords in *Smith v Eric S Bush* (1989) which also concerned the liability of surveyors in respect of building society valuations. The claimant purchaser was able to rely on the valuation despite the inclusion of a disclaimer in the report. The disclaimer was not reasonable under the **Unfair Contract Terms Act 1977**. These cases are authority for property of a modest value. Lord Griffiths said:

> I have come to the conclusion that Yianni's case was correctly decided…In the case of a surveyor valuing a small house for a building society or local authority, the application of these three criteria leads to the conclusion that he owed a duty of care to the purchaser. If the valuation is negligent and is relied on, damage in the form of economic loss to the purchaser is obviously foreseeable. The necessary proximity arises from the surveyor's knowledge that the overwhelming probability is that the purchaser will rely on his valuation, the evidence was that surveyors knew that approximately 90% of purchasers did so, and the fact that the surveyor only obtains the work because the purchaser is willing to pay his fee. It is just and reasonable that the duty should be imposed, for the advice is given in a professional as opposed to a social context and liability for breach of the duty will be limited both as to its extent and amount. The extent of the liability is

limited to the purchaser of the house: I would not extend it to subsequent purchasers. The amount of the liability cannot be very great because it relates to a modest house.

3 The reliance must be reasonable

The courts seem to regard such reliance as reasonable where it is foreseeable. In *Caparo* v *Dickman* (1990), the House of Lords gave guidelines as to when reliance may be foreseeable/reasonable. The defendant auditors were held not to be liable to the claimants for the negligent preparation of accounts. The claimants relied on the accounts to purchase further shares and eventually to take over the company. The accounts were inaccurate and misleading, and the claimants consequently incurred financial loss. Lord Bridge, having considered the relevant case law said:

> The salient feature of all these cases is that the defendant giving advice or information was fully aware of the nature of the transaction which the claimant had in contemplation, knew that the advice or information would be communicated to him directly or indirectly and knew that it was very likely that the claimant would rely on that advice or information in deciding whether or not to engage in the transaction in contemplation.

However, in this case it was held that there was insufficient proximity between the auditors and the company's shareholders.

Soon after this decision, the case of *James McNaughton Papers Group Ltd* v *Hicks Anderson and Co* (1991) was heard by the Court of Appeal. Bearing similar facts to *Caparo* v *Dickman*, the defendants were accountants who prepared accounts at short notice for the chairman of a company. The accounts were then shown to the claimants, who relied on them to their detriment in bidding for and taking over the company. Neill LJ identified a number of factors that are important in ascertaining whether a duty of care exists:
- the purpose for which the statement is made
- the purpose for which the statement is communicated
- the relationship between the advisor, the advisee and any relevant third party
- the size of any class to which the advisee belongs
- the state of knowledge of the advisor
- reliance by the advisee

Here the Court of Appeal found that no duty was owed to the claimants as the draft accounts were not prepared for their benefit, and the defendant would reasonably expect a party to a take-over bid to take independent advice.

Limiting the circumstances

Words have a greater propensity than physical articles to spread, and, to quote Cardozo CJ in *Ultramares Corpn* v *Touche* (1931), could subject the maker of the statement to 'liability in an indeterminate amount for an indeterminate time to an indeterminate class'. The judiciary has, therefore, limited the circumstances in which the makers of negligent misstatements will be liable to compensate those people whom they cause to suffer economic loss. In *Hedley Byrne*, Lord Reid stated:

Another obvious difference is that a negligently made article will only cause one accident, and so it is not very difficult to find the necessary degree of proximity or neighbourhood between the negligent manufacturer and the person injured. But words can be broadcast with or without the consent or the foresight of the speaker or writer. It would be one thing to say that the speaker owed a duty to a limited class, but it would be going very far to say that he owed a duty to every ultimate 'consumer' who acts on those words to his detriment.

The extended Hedley Byrne principle

In addition to the courts permitting the recovery in negligence of economic loss arising from personal injury, damage to property or a negligent misstatement, there are some circumstances in which liability has been imposed that do not fall squarely within these exceptions to the general rule against recovery. There does not appear to be a consistent principle applied in these circumstances, although recently there has been an attempt to fit them into the so-called 'extended Hedley Byrne principle'.

The difficulty has usually arisen in cases where the courts have clearly been in favour of imposing liability but there is an absence of reliance on the part of the claimant. This was the problem facing the courts in the so-called 'wills cases'. In *Ross* v *Caunters* (1979), a solicitor prepared a will but failed to ensure that it was appropriately witnessed. The will was witnessed by the spouse of the beneficiary and this resulted in the legacy being void. The claimant/would-be beneficiary successfully sued the solicitor for the economic loss sustained, despite having herself not acted in reliance on the solicitor. Sir Robert Megarry VC described the basis of the solicitor's liability to others as 'either an extension of the Hedley Byrne principle or, more probably, a direct application of the principle in *Donoghue* v *Stevenson*'. He further explained that where a solicitor is instructed to carry out a transaction that benefits a third party, that third party is clearly within contemplation as being likely to be affected, and the fact that the loss is purely financial should be no bar to a claim.

Sixteen years later, the House of Lords approved this decision in *White* v *Jones* (1995). A testator had cut his daughters out of his estate following a quarrel. There was then reconciliation between the testator and his daughters and he instructed the solicitor to prepare a new will, including a £9,000 legacy to each of the daughters. The solicitor failed to act on the instructions before the testator died. The daughters' claim that the solicitor owed them a duty of care in these circumstances succeeded. Lord Goff gave the leading judgement. The problem in not allowing this type of claim would be that the testator and his/her estate would have a valid claim but suffer no loss, while the disappointed beneficiary would have suffered loss but have no claim. This would result in no potential claim against a negligent solicitor. This issue was described as being 'a point of cardinal importance in the present case'. Lord Goff said that under the Hedley Byrne principle, the assumption of responsibility by the solicitor to the client should, in law, be held to extend to the intended beneficiary to prevent the beneficiary being deprived of his/her legacy in circumstances where neither the testator nor his estate has a remedy against the solicitor.

In *Spring* v *Guardian Assurance* (1994), the issue arose again as to whether there was reliance by the claimant. The question for the House of Lords was whether an employer owes a duty of care to an employee when providing a reference for a prospective future employer. Hedley Byrne established that a duty of care was owed to the recipient of the reference but the claimant was the subject of the reference and could not be said to have acted in reliance on its content. In this case, the defendant employer suggested in the reference that the employee was dishonest and had little integrity. Lord Goff, however, had little difficulty in finding for the claimant on the basis of Hedley Byrne. He pointed out that the employer is possessed of special knowledge of the employee due to experience of his/her performance. Furthermore, such references are provided not only for the assistance of the prospective employer, but also for the assistance of the employee in securing employment, and the employee therefore relies on the employer to take care in the preparation of the reference.

There is a lack of consistency in the approach of the judiciary in these cases. Lord Goff justified his decision in *White* v *Jones* on the basis of an assumption of responsibility being fundamental to a special relationship and did not consider the issue of reliance. In *Spring*, he again referred to the assumption of responsibility on the part of the employer but addressed the issue of reliance. Lord Slynn and Lord Woolf, however, did not mention assumption of responsibility but did agree that there was a sufficiently close relationship to impose liability.

There has been considerable academic criticism of the above decisions and of the attempt to promote the 'assumption of responsibility test' as important in establishing a special relationship. However, there does seem to be considerable judicial agreement, albeit not shared by the dissenting judges, that there is a need to extend the Hedley Byrne principle to provide justice where it would otherwise be denied. Lord Goff in *White* v *Jones* was influenced by what he said was 'the impulse to do practical justice'. Similarly, in *Williams* v *Natural Life Health Foods Ltd* (1998) Lord Steyn justified the extension of the Hedley Byrne principle on the basis that 'coherence must sometimes yield to practical justice'. However, in this particular case, the claim was unsuccessful due to there being no direct or indirect assumption of responsibility by the defendant and no reliance by the claimant. The overall effect of these cases is that the principle of Hedley Byrne has now been extended in limited circumstances to the provision of services, including services provided for the benefit of a third party, and reliance is not crucial to the existence of a special relationship. As Lord Steyn stated in *Williams*: 'The extended Hedley Byrne principle is the rationalisation or technique adopted by English law for the recovery of damages in respect of economic loss caused by the negligent performance of services.'

Occupiers' liability

Before the **Occupiers' Liability Act 1957** was passed, occupiers' liability was dealt with by common law. The law relating to occupiers was complicated because different levels of care were owed to the various categories of claimant. However, the law has now been greatly simplified by means of codification in the **Occupiers' Liability Acts of 1957 and 1984**.

The Occupiers' Liability Act 1957 — the duty owed to lawful visitors

Who is the occupier?

Section 1(2) of the 1957 Act states that the persons who are to be treated as the occupier are the same as the persons who would in common law have been treated as the occupier. The common-law position is illustrated by *Wheat v Lacon* (1966). Here, the owners of a pub employed a manager who lived on the premises and who was authorised to take lodgers. One lodger was injured while using an unlit staircase. The House of Lords held that the owners could still be sued as occupiers because they retained some control over the state of the premises. Lord Denning, delivering the leading judgement, went on to explain that the manager was also an occupier, as he had a considerable degree of control over the premises. It is therefore possible for two or more people to be occupiers. This question of 'control' is crucial, and in each case is a question of fact to be decided by the judge.

To whom is the duty owed?

The **Occupiers' Liability Act 1957** abolished the common-law distinction between various categories of entrant and created instead a single category of 'lawful visitors'. A lawful visitor is anyone who is present on the premises by the occupier's invitation, or with the occupier's express or implied permission, or in exercise of a legal right. This would include people who have received an invitation and those who have paid for the right of entry, e.g. to a theatre or theme park. Those who visit as a result of implied permission include meter readers, delivery people or the fire brigade summoned to deal with a fire. Lawful authority also covers the police and others exercising rights granted by warrant. Casual visitors, e.g. political canvassers and door-to-door salespeople, are also included, following the general rule that any person has the right to come as far as the front door unless steps are taken to prevent this, such as a locked gate or warning notice. Interestingly, people who use a right of way are not considered to be visitors and accordingly are not owed a duty of care. This was confirmed in *McGeown v Northern Ireland Housing Executive* (1995).

The invitation or permission may be issued by someone other than the occupier. The occupier's wife, husband or children may invite a friend into the family home, and permission to enter commercial premises does not normally require the express authority of the board of directors. A more difficult situation arises where an employee, or junior member of the family, violates an express instruction not to allow visitors. In *Stone* v *Taffe* (1974), a pub manager had been instructed not to let friends remain on the premises after closing time, except for a bona fide private party notified in advance to the brewery and the police. He ignored this instruction, and a guest fell on unlit stairs. The brewery was held liable. The guest was a lawful visitor since he did not know of the prohibition and believed he was on the premises by invitation.

Where is the duty owed?

The 1957 Act imposes a duty on occupiers of premises. The term 'premises' is given a broad meaning by s.1(3), and may be 'any fixed or movable structure, including any vessel, vehicle or aircraft'.

Besides covering houses, buildings and the land itself, premises have also been held to include:
- ships in dry dock (*London Graving Dock* v *Horton*, 1951)
- vehicles (*Hartwell* v *Grayson*, 1947)
- lifts (*Haseldine* v *Daw and Son Ltd*, 1941)
- ladders (*Wheeler* v *Copas*, 1981)

What is the duty owed?

Section 2(1) provides that the duty owed is the common-law duty of care, which is stated in s.2(2) as being:

> ...a duty to take such care as in all the circumstances of the case is reasonable to see that the visitor will be reasonably safe in using the premises for the purposes for which he is invited or permitted by the occupier to be there.

The duty is not absolute but requires the occupier to take reasonable care. The occupier will be judged by the negligence standard, the standard of the 'reasonable man'. Liability of the occupier is dependent on whether he has or has not done what the reasonable person would have or would not have done.

In *Martin* v *Middlesbrough Corporation* (1965), a school girl slipped in the playground and cut herself on a broken milk bottle. The council was held liable because it had not made adequate arrangements for disposing of the bottle. In *Cunningham* v *Reading FC* (1991), a football club was liable to police officers injured by lumps of concrete thrown by visiting Bristol City fans. The club knew from past experience that the visiting crowd was likely to contain a violent element that had thrown concrete on a previous visit some 4 months earlier, but had made no effort to remove or repair the loose concrete, in spite of the relatively low cost of doing so.

The duty is, however, limited in that it is only owed in respect of the purpose for which the visitor is permitted to be on the premises. No duty is owed under the Act to entrants who use the premises for other purposes. As Lord Scrutton LJ said in *The Calgarth* (1927): 'When you invite a person into your house to use the stairs, you do not invite him to slide down the banisters.' Entrants who exceed the scope of the occupiers' permission become non-visitors under the 1984 Act in the event that they suffer injury.

The duty owed to children

Section 2(3)(a) provides that an occupier must be prepared for children to be less careful than adults, so the premises must be reasonably safe for a child.

The reasoning for this is that what may pose no threat to an adult may nevertheless be dangerous to a child. In *Moloney* v *Lambeth LBC* (1966), a 4-year-old fell through a gap in a railing guarding a stairwell and was injured. An adult could not have fallen through the gap, so such an injury would have been impossible for an adult. The occupier was held liable.

Similarly, a child is unlikely to appreciate risks as an adult would, and may be attracted to danger. Consequently, an occupier should guard against any kind of allurement that places a child visitor at risk of harm. In *Glasgow Corporation* v *Taylor* (1922), a 7-year-old ate poisonous berries in a botanical garden and died. The shrub on which the berries grew was not fenced off in any way. The Corporation was held liable as it knew that the berries were poisonous and should have expected that a young child might be attracted to the shrub. The same approach was taken in *Jolley* v *Sutton LBC* (2000). The House of Lords restored the decision of the trial judge in holding the defendant liable to a 14-year-old boy, who was seriously injured when an old boat fell on him. The boat was something that would be attractive to children, including those of the claimant's age, and some injury was foreseeable if children played in or around it.

The courts will sometimes take the view that very young children should be under their parents' supervision. In such circumstances the occupier will not be liable. In *Phipps* v *Rochester Corporation* (1955), a 5-year-old was injured having fallen down a trench dug by the defendant on a piece of waste ground where the child frequently played. The defendant was not liable because the court held that the parents should have had the child under proper control. The Corporation had granted only 'conditional licence' to children accompanied by an adult.

The duty owed to experts

Section 2(3)(b) provides that an occupier may expect that a person in the exercise of his/her calling will appreciate and guard against any special risks ordinarily incidental to it.

Where tradespeople fail to guard against risks that they should know about, the occupier will not be liable. In *Roles* v *Nathan* (1963), the occupier was not liable when chimney sweeps died after inhaling carbon monoxide fumes while cleaning flues. The sweeps did not accept the advice of the occupiers to complete the work with boilers off and, in any case, should have been aware of the risks themselves. The occupier may not, however, expect experts to guard against risks not incidental to their trade. Lord Denning in this case pointed out that the outcome would have been different if the sweeps had been killed by a basement staircase giving way, as such a risk is not incidental to cleaning chimneys.

Furthermore, the occupier may not expect experts to exercise more than the usual safeguards particular to their trade to guard against risks that are created by the occupier's own negligence. In *Ogwo* v *Taylor* (1987), a householder who started a fire by his careless use of a blowlamp was liable for injuries suffered by a fireman while fighting the fire. The risk was one that the fireman could not effectively guard against. Similarly, in *Salmon* v *Seafarer* (1983) the owners of a restaurant were liable. They had failed to turn off a chip fryer, which then started a fire and injured the defendant fireman who was fighting it.

For what damage may the occupier be held liable?

Section 1(3)(b) states that the Act applies not only to personal injury and death but also to damage to property, including property that does not belong to the visitor.

Warnings

Section 2(4)(a) provides that the occupier's liability is discharged if he/she gives effective warning of the danger. The warning must be sufficient to enable the visitor to be reasonably safe. In *Roles* v *Nathan*, Lord Denning explained the provisions of s.2(4)(a):

> Supposing, for instance, that there was only one way of getting into and out of premises and it was by a footbridge over a stream which was rotten and dangerous. An occupier puts up a notice: 'This bridge is dangerous.' In such a case, s.2(4)(a) makes it clear that the occupier would nowadays be liable. But if there were two footbridges, one of which was rotten, and the other safe 100 yards away, the occupier could still escape liability, even today by putting up a notice 'Do not use this footbridge. It is dangerous. There is a safe one further upstream'. Such a warning is sufficient because it does enable the visitor to be reasonably safe.

In some circumstances, a mere warning may be insufficient to safeguard the visitor, and the occupier may be obliged to set up barriers. A warning was ineffective in respect of a deep pit inside the entrance of a dark shed in *Rae* v *Mars Ltd* (1990). The occupier was liable.

There is, however, no specific obligation to display a warning notice when the danger is one that should be obvious to any visitor. In *Cotton* v *Derbyshire Dales* (1994), a walker was injured after falling from a high path along dangerous cliffs in a much-visited area. There was no notice warning of the danger. The Court of Appeal said the absence of a notice was not a breach of the common duty of care. The danger was obvious to visitors exercising reasonable care for their own safety.

Negligence of independent contractors

Under s.2(4)(b), the occupier will not be liable for loss or injuries suffered by his or her visitors when the cause of damage is the negligence of an independent contractor hired by the occupier. The reasoning behind this subsection is that the contractor will be covered by his or her own insurance.

There are two requirements that must be met for this section to apply:

1 It must be reasonable for the occupier to have entrusted the work to the independent contractor. In *Haseldine* v *Daw* (1941), the occupier was not liable for the negligent repair of a lift as this was a job requiring specialist skills.

2 The occupier must take reasonable steps to satisfy himself or herself that the contractor was competent and that the work has been properly completed. Only reasonable steps must be taken. If the work is of a highly complex and technical nature, it is less reasonable to impose this obligation. However, if the risk is obvious then the occupier will be expected to discover it. In *Woodward* v *The Mayor of Hastings* (1945), the occupiers were liable when a child was injured on school steps, which were negligently left icy after the contractors had cleaned off snow. The risk should have been obvious to the occupiers. Similarly, in *Bottomley* v *Todmorden Cricket Club* (2003), the claimant was injured while helping with a fireworks display on the cricket club's land, organised by an independent contractor. The club argued that since the display was organised by independent contractors, albeit for the club's benefit, it had no liability under the 1957 Act. Dismissing the cricket club's appeal, Brooke LJ said an occupier in such circumstances can usually escape liability by showing that he has taken reasonable care to select competent and safe contractors. In the instant case, however, there was no written safety plan and the cricket club had not insisted that the independent contractor take out adequate public liability insurance.

Excluding liability

Under s.2(1), the occupier can extend, restrict, modify and exclude liability to his or her visitors. However, the exclusion clauses are subject to restrictions and will not apply:

- in the case of strangers, for example a tenant's visitors, because they will have had no opportunity to agree to the exclusion
- against children, who may be unable to read or to fully understand their implications
- in respect of death or personal injury caused by the occupier's breach of duty under the 1957 Act by virtue of the **Unfair Contract Terms Act 1977**; this restriction applies where the premises are occupied for the business purposes of the occupier

Defences

The occupier may raise the general defences of contributory negligence and *volenti non fit injuria*.

Contributory negligence

Under the **Law Reform (Contributory Negligence) Act 1945**, damages are reduced according to the claimant's responsibility for the damage suffered.

Volenti non fit injuria

The risk must be fully understood by the visitor. In *Simms* v *Leigh RFC* (1960), a visiting rugby player was tackled near the edge of the pitch, collided with a concrete wall and broke a leg. The wall was 7 feet 3 inches from the touchline. League regulations stated it should be at least 7 feet away. The judge found as fact that it was not proven that the injury had resulted from the collision with the wall, and it could have been from the tackle alone. However, *in obiter* the judge said that even if causation had been proven, the claimant had been *volenti* to the risk of injury on a ground laid out in accordance with league rules. There would thus be no liability when the injury was sustained within the normal rules of the game.

Mere knowledge of the risk is insufficient. The risk must be accepted. In *White* v *Blackmore* (1972), general knowledge that jalopy racing was dangerous did not mean that the claimant had accepted inadequate safety arrangements.

The claimant must freely choose to consent. In *Burnett* v *British Waterways Board* (1973), a claimant on a barge entering the defendant's dry dock had no choice but to be there. The defence of consent was therefore unavailable.

The Occupiers' Liability Act 1984 — the duty owed to trespassers

The **Occupiers' Liability Act 1984** was passed to clarify the law relating to categories of claimant not covered by the 1957 Act. The harshness of the judicial approach in *Addie* v *Dumbreck* (1929), whereby the occupier's duty was to refrain from causing deliberate or reckless injury, was to some extent mitigated by the decision of the House of Lords in *British Railways Board* v *Herrington* (1972). A young boy was injured when he gained access to an electrified railway line through vandalised fencing. Lord Diplock said the duty owed to a trespasser was limited to taking reasonable steps, as would be taken by a man of ordinary humane feeling, to enable the trespasser to avoid the danger. This duty became known as 'the duty of common humanity'.

Following the *Herrington* decision, the question of liability to trespassers was referred to the Law Commission and its report in 1976 subsequently formed the basis of the **Occupiers' Liability Act 1984**.

Who is the occupier?

Section 1(2) of the 1984 Act states that the word 'occupier' bears the same meaning as under the **Occupiers' Liability Act 1957**. An occupier under the 1984 Act will thus, as stated by Lord Denning in *Wheat* v *Lacon* (1966), be a person who has a sufficient degree of control over the premises.

To whom is the duty owed?

Section 1(1) of the 1984 Act states that the duty is owed to persons other than visitors. Under s.1(2) of the 1984 Act, it is provided that the word 'visitor' bears the same meaning as under the **Occupiers' Liability Act 1957**. The 1984 Act is clearly intended to provide for those categories of entrant not provided for under the 1957 Act. Usually, entrants covered by the 1984 Act will be trespassers. However, the Act also applies to people who, without the permission of the occupier, are involuntarily on the premises, and to persons exercising a private right of way, and to members of the public entering under an access order or agreement made under the **National Parks and Access to the Countryside Act 1949**.

It is expressly provided by s.1(7) that the 1984 Act does not apply to persons using the highway. Users of highways maintained at public expense are regulated by the **Highways Act 1980** (which is beyond the scope of the AQA specification).

Where is the duty owed?

The duty is owed by the occupier of premises. Under s.1(2) of the 1984 Act, premises are stated as including any fixed or movable structure. Section 1(9) defines 'movable structure' as including any vessel, vehicle or aircraft. The meaning of premises is thus the same as under the 1957 Act.

In what circumstances is the duty owed?

In *Herrington* v *British Railways Board* (1972), the Law Lords gave differing accounts of the circumstances in which the duty of common humanity was owed. These circumstances are now clarified in the 1984 Act. Section 1(3) states that an occupier of premises owes a duty to a non-visitor if:

(a) he/she is aware of the danger or has reasonable grounds to believe that it exists

(b) he/she knows or has reasonable grounds to believe that the other is in the vicinity of the danger concerned or that the other may come into the vicinity of the danger, and

(c) the risk is one against which, in all the circumstances of the case, he/she may reasonably be expected to offer the other some protection

Both (a) and (b) are subjective, i.e. they relate to the knowledge of the defendant. If the defendant is unaware of the danger or unaware that the person may come onto the premises, then he/she will not be liable, notwithstanding that such facts would be obvious to the reasonable person. In *Swain* v *Natui Ram Pun* (1996), a boy trespassing on the roof of the defendant's factory fell off and was seriously injured. Dismissing his claim, the court said the factory was surrounded by substantial fences and there was no evidence of previous trespass. Therefore, the defendant had no reasonable grounds to believe there was anyone in the vicinity of the danger. In *obiter*,

Pill LJ said that s.1(3)(b) imposes a subjective test based on the occupier's actual knowledge of facts giving such grounds, not on what he/she ought to have known.

The effect of this subsection is also illustrated by *White* v *St Albans DC* (1990). The claimant fell into a trench while taking a short cut across the defendant's land. He argued that the fact that the council had fenced the land showed it was aware of the risk of trespass, so satisfying the requirement of s.1(3)(b). In dismissing this argument, the Court of Appeal upheld the decision of the trial judge. The provision of fencing was not a common occurrence, and was therefore not evidence that the defendant believed the claimant was likely to enter onto its land.

However, the third requirement (c) is both subjective and objective. The focus is on 'all the circumstances of the case', which may include the purpose of the entry, the age and capabilities of the non-visitor and the financial resources of the occupier. The majority of the House of Lords in *Herrington* were of the opinion that the financial resources of the occupier should be considered. They were also of the view that the circumstances in which the duty was owed should be based on the knowledge of the occupier.

What is the duty owed?

Section 1(4) states that the duty owed by an occupier to a non-visitor is 'to take such care as is reasonable in all the circumstances of the case to see that he does not suffer injury on the premises by reason of the danger concerned'.

In respect of what damage is the duty owed?

Section 1(1) states that the duty owed under the 1984 Act applies in respect of injury. In s.1(9), 'injury' is defined as meaning death or personal injury, including disease and any impairment of physical or mental condition. By virtue of s.1(8), the 1984 Act does not apply in respect of damage to property.

Warnings

Section 1(5) states that the occupier may discharge his or her duty by 'taking such steps as are reasonable in all the circumstances of the case to give warning of the danger concerned or to discourage persons from incurring the risk'.

The level of warning required to discharge the occupier's duty under the 1984 Act is therefore lower than that required under the 1957 Act. The 1984 Act does not require the warning to be sufficient to enable the entrant to be safe in remaining on the premises. Rather, the emphasis is on making the potential entrant aware of why he/she should not come onto the premises.

Excluding liability

The Law Commission, in its 1976 report, expressly provided that occupiers should be able to exclude liability to non-visitors, subject to the exclusion satisfying the requirement of reasonableness. However, no mention of exclusion is made in the 1984 Act. As the 1957 Act specifically mentions circumstances in which the duty to visitors can be excluded, and as the 1984 Act in s.2 amends the **Unfair Contract Terms Act 1977** in respect of the scope of business liability of occupiers, it may be concluded that the duty imposed on occupiers in respect of non-visitors is intended to be non-excludable.

Defences

The occupier may raise the general defences of contributory negligence and *volenti non fit injuria*.

Contributory negligence

Under the **Law Reform (Contributory Negligence) Act 1945**, damages are reduced according to the claimant's responsibility for the damage suffered.

Volenti non fit injuria

The defence of *volenti non fit injuria* is expressly provided for by s.1(6), which states that 'no duty is owed to a person in respect of risks which he willingly accepts as his'.

In *Ratcliff* v *McConnell* (1998), a 19-year-old student climbed over a locked gate late one night and dived into the swimming pool that was closed for the winter and partially drained. He dived into the shallow end and hit his head on the bottom, sustaining serious injuries. He sued the defendant under the 1984 Act and the trial judge found in his favour subject to a deduction for contributory negligence. Allowing the defendant's appeal, Stuart-Smith LJ said there were several warning notices around the pool, and the dangers of diving into water of unknown depth were too well known to need any further express warning. The claimant had accepted the risks, and under s.1(6) of the 1984 Act his claim must fail.

Nuisance

Nuisance can be classified under three headings: private, public and statutory. This guide covers private and public nuisance, in accordance with the AQA specification.

Private nuisance

Professor Winfield in *Winfield and Jolowicz on Tort*, defines private nuisance as 'unlawful interference with a person's use or enjoyment of land, or some right over, or in connection with it'.

Unlawful interference

Not all interference with enjoyment of land will constitute a nuisance. Such interference will only be unlawful if it is unreasonable. The law of nuisance thus allows for give and take. Lord Wright commented in *Sedleigh-Denfield* v *O'Callaghan* (1940): 'A balance has to be maintained between the right of the occupier to do what he likes with his own land, and the right of his neighbour not to be interfered with.' The interference will not constitute a nuisance unless it is substantial, 'not merely according to elegant or dainty modes and habits of living, but according to plain and sober and simple notions among the English people' (Knight-Bruce in *Walter* v *Selfe*, 1851).

Reasonableness in nuisance is different from the reasonableness element of negligence. In negligence, the reasonableness of the defendant's conduct is the central issue. However, in nuisance the central issue is the reasonableness of the outcome of the defendant's conduct. The focus of a nuisance action is thus on the reasonableness of the interference caused to the claimant. The defendant cannot argue as a defence that he/she took reasonable care. However, the conduct of the defendant is relevant in circumstances where he/she has acted maliciously.

In deciding whether the interference is unreasonable, the courts will take into account various factors:
- the nature of the locality
- the sensitivity of the claimant
- the motive or malice of the defendant
- the interference must be ongoing

The nature of the locality
In an industrial area, fumes will be less likely to be considered unlawful interference than in a rural area. Pollock J stated in *Bamford* v *Turnley* (1865): 'That may be a nuisance in Grosvenor Square which would be none in Smithfield market.' In a residential area, cocks crowing in the morning will be more likely to be considered unlawful interference than in a rural area. In *Leeman* v *Montague* (1936), the claimant lived in a largely residential area and was regularly disturbed by the crowing of 750 cockerels on the defendant's land, approximately 100 yards away. The court held that this constituted a nuisance.

However, if there is physical damage to the claimant's property, the locality issue will not absolve the defendant from liability. In *St Helens Smelting Co* v *Tipping* (1865), the claimant bought an estate near the defendants' smelting works and suffered damage to his trees and other crops caused by the fumes. The defendants argued that there were many other smelting works in the area and so the nature of the locality prevented the interference from being unlawful. Lord Westbury LC said surrounding circumstances were relevant where enjoyment was concerned, but not where there was material damage. The claimant's action succeeded.

The sensitivity of the claimant
A claimant cannot put his land to an unusually delicate use and then complain when his land is adversely affected by his neighbour's activities to a greater extent than would usually be the case. Note in this respect the words of Knight-Bruce regarding 'elegant or dainty modes and habits of living'. In *Amphitheatres Inc* v *Portland Meadows*

(1948), the claimant's action failed when his drive-in cinema was affected by the defendant's floodlit premises.

Similarly, in *Robinson* v *Kilvert* (1889), the claimant's unusually sensitive brown paper was damaged when the defendant heated his cellar, thus raising the temperature of the claimant's premises. The defendant was not liable as normal brown paper would not have been affected.

The motive or malice of the defendant
Where the defendant's activity is motivated by malice, the courts are likely to hold such activity to be unlawful. In *Christy* v *Davey* (1893), the claimant gave music lessons for approximately 17 hours per week. This annoyed her neighbour who lived in the adjoining semi-detached house. He retaliated by banging trays on the wall, shouting and blowing whistles. The claimant was successful as the defendant had acted deliberately and maliciously.

When the activity is motivated by malice, the defendant cannot argue that the claimant is unusually sensitive. In *Hollywood Silver Fox Farm* v *Emmett* (1936), the defendant discharged his gun on his own property but close to the claimant's land in order to frighten the plaintiff's silver fox breeding vixen, causing her to miscarry. Despite the delicate use of land by the claimant, the defendant's malicious intention rendered his actions a nuisance.

The interference must be ongoing
The law of nuisance is concerned with activities that are ongoing, i.e. a state of affairs. However, the courts have at times held that seemingly one-off incidents are a nuisance. They have done this by finding that the preceding state of the defendant's land constituted the nuisance.

In *Spicer* v *Smee* (1949), the claimant succeeded in nuisance when his home was destroyed by fire caused by defective wiring in the defendant's home. The defective wiring was the state of affairs.

A further example is provided by *British Celanese Ltd* v *A. H. Hunt (Capacitors) Ltd* (1969). The defendants collected metal strips as part of their business. These metal strips were blown about by the wind and some landed on an electricity substation causing a power failure to the claimant's factory. The defendants were held liable, the collection of metal strips on their land being the state of affairs.

Who can sue?

Anyone with a proprietary interest in the land may bring an action in nuisance. This will usually be the occupier, but may be a landlord who is out of possession. Members of the occupier's family cannot sue (but may sue, e.g. in negligence if there is personal injury or damage to property).

An early example of this principle is provided by *Malone* v *Laskey* (1907). Mrs Malone and her husband occupied property provided by the husband's employers and sublet from Laskey who operated an engine in adjoining premises. The vibrations that the engine created caused a bracket supporting a water tank in the Malone's house to collapse and injure Mrs Malone. Although the working of the engine was a nuisance, Mrs Malone's action failed as she had no proprietary interest in the property. (This case would be decided differently today, as wives now have statutory occupation rights.)

The principle established in *Malone* was upset in *Khorasandjian* v *Bush* (1993). The claimant, a young woman living with her parents, was receiving unwanted telephone calls and being otherwise harassed by a former boyfriend. In upholding the decision of the court of first instance, the Court of Appeal held that the claimant, as an occupier of property, had a right to bring an action in nuisance, notwithstanding that she had no legal or equitable interest in the land affected. However, the House of Lords in *Hunter* v *Canary Wharf* (1997) reaffirmed the principle of *Malone* v *Laskey*. Lord Goff said the idea that the claimant need only a 'substantial link' with the property affected, as suggested by the Court of Appeal, was too vague, and would transform nuisance from a tort against land into a tort against the person.

The damage suffered must be of a foreseeable type

The claimant may recover damages for any foreseeable loss that he/she has suffered as a result of the nuisance. The House of Lords in *Cambridge Water* v *Eastern Counties Leather* (1994) held that the loss suffered must be of a type that was reasonably foreseeable. Lord Goff said:

> It by no means follows that the defendant should be liable for damage of a type which he could not foresee; and the development of the law of negligence in the past 60 years points strongly towards a requirement that such foreseeability be a prerequisite of liability in damages for nuisance, as it is of liability in negligence.

No liability in private nuisance for personal injury

Damages for personal injury are not recoverable per se in private nuisance. In *Hunter* v *Canary Wharf*, the House of Lords reasserted the principle that nuisance is a tort against land and not a tort against the person.

Who can be sued?

Anyone who causes a nuisance is liable for its creation and continuance. If the nuisance emanates from land, the occupier is primarily liable, and the owner not in occupation is liable only if he/she was the person who created or authorised the nuisance. An occupier is responsible for nuisances created by his/her employees, agent, family, guests and independent contractors. This is an exception to the general principle that employers are not liable for their independent contractors. In *Hole* v *Sittingbourne Railway* (1861), the independent contractor built a swing bridge so badly that it would not open. The defendant employer was held liable. Similarly, in *Matania* v *NP Bank Ltd* (1937), the defendants were held liable for the nuisance created by the noisy building operations of their independent contractor.

Remedies

A person disturbed by a private nuisance has four main remedies open to him/her:

- damages
- an injunction
- abatement
- a complaint to the local council

Damages

In a nuisance action, damages will often be an inadequate remedy and will not usually be awarded alone where the nuisance is likely to continue. In *Tetley* v *Chitty* (1986), a local council gave permission for the operation of a go-kart track on council-owned land. Three neighbours sought an injunction. McNeill J held the noise to be an inevitable consequence of the use for which permission had been given, so that the council was liable in private nuisance. Damages would have been wholly insufficient as a remedy, and an injunction was granted to restrain the council from permitting this activity.

Damages may be awarded where the damage done by the nuisance is quantifiable. Damages for past loss or inconvenience may also be awarded, together with an injunction to restrain any further nuisance. In *Hollywood Silver Fox Farm v Emmett* (see page 41) the judge awarded damages and an injunction restraining the defendant from firing guns or making other noises near the fox farm during the breeding season.

Injunctions

An injunction is usually the preferred remedy for the claimant, since it requires the defendant to bring the nuisance to an end. It also has the advantage of flexibility, in that it can be tailored to meet the exact circumstances of the case and produce a just solution (often a compromise). In *Leeman* v *Montague* (1936), the claimant bought a house in a largely residential area, and was regularly disturbed from 2 a.m. onwards by the crowing of 750 cockerels in the defendant's orchard, approximately 100 yards away. The court held this activity to be a nuisance and granted an injunction restraining the defendant from carrying on his business in this manner. There was evidence suggesting that the defendant could easily rearrange the use of his land to keep the birds further away from the houses. Similarly, in *Kennaway* v *Thompson* (1980) the owners of a number of lakeside homes complained of the noise caused by power-boat racing on the lake. Lawton LJ granted an injunction against the organisers of the racing, limiting both the number of days on which racing could take place and the number and power of boats allowed to take part.

It must be remembered that the injunction is an equitable remedy and, as such, available at the discretion of the court. Where the claimant seeks an injunction, the court may decide to award damages instead if an injunction would not be in the public interest. In *Miller* v *Jackson* (1977), the claimant bought a house overlooking the village cricket ground. Cricket balls were frequently hit into her garden. The claimant sought an injunction. The Court of Appeal held the activity to constitute a nuisance but declined to grant an injunction on the basis that it would not be in the public interest to prevent the public playing cricket. Damages of £400 were awarded to cover both past and future inconvenience.

Similarly, the public interest outweighed the private interest in the more recent case of *Dennis* v *Ministry of Defence* (2003) (unreported). The claimants lived with their three teenage children directly below the flight path of RAF Harrier jets used in pilot training. They sought an injunction in respect of the excessive noise. After hearing evidence that the noise level was very high, Buckley J awarded the claimants damages totalling almost £1 million, including £300,000 for the loss of value to their home. The public interest in maintaining the training programme at the RAF station was greater than the claimants' private interest. However, selected individuals should not bear the cost of the public benefit, and common fairness demanded that the claimants should be compensated.

Abatement

Abatement is a form of self-help. The claimant is entitled to take steps to alleviate the nuisance, for example by cutting off the roots or branches of the defendant's tree that encroach onto his/her property. The claimant is even entitled, after giving due notice (except in an emergency) to enter onto the defendant's land to abate the nuisance, so long as he/she does no more damage than is strictly necessary for his/her purpose. In *Lemmon* v *Webb* (1895), branches from the claimant's trees were overhanging the defendant's land. When the defendant cut them off the claimant sought damages. The House of Lords held that, although a person must normally give notice before taking steps to abate a nuisance, this is not necessary in an emergency or if (as here) he/she can take the necessary steps without leaving his/her own land.

Complaints to the local authority

Under s.79 of the **Environmental Protection Act 1990**, a local authority has a duty to investigate any complaints of a statutory nuisance, including anything prejudicial to health, or causing a nuisance arising from the state of premises, or any accumulation or deposit thereon, or smoke, fumes, gas, dust, steam, smells or noise emitted from them, or from any animal kept in an unsuitable place or manner. The local authority can issue an abatement order, directing the occupier to eliminate the nuisance. Failure to comply is punishable by a fine, with an additional penalty for each day the nuisance continues. This procedure does not allow the aggrieved neighbour to recover damages, but may in some cases be more effective in securing compliance than an individual civil action.

Public nuisance

Professor Rogers states: 'The essence of a public nuisance is that it is something which affects the comfort and convenience of the public as a whole rather than of an individual complainant.'

Class of people

The nuisance must affect a class of people. Romer LJ in *A-G v PYA Quarries* (1957) stated that the nuisance would affect a class of people if it were 'so widespread in its range or indiscriminate in its effects that it would not be reasonable to expect one person to take steps to put a stop to it'. In this case, quarrying operations of the defendants, causing vibrations and dust to affect houses in the vicinity, were held to be a public nuisance.

Public nuisance is a criminal offence

In *R v Johnson* (1996), the defendant was convicted of public nuisance in respect of several hundred obscene telephone calls made to more than a dozen women over a period of 6 years. Upholding his conviction, Tucker J said a single call would have been a private rather than a public nuisance, but cumulatively the calls materially affected the reasonable comfort and convenience of a class of Her Majesty's subjects. The jury, properly directed, had decided that the women were sufficient in number to constitute such a class.

Public nuisance most often arises on the highway

In *Attorney General v Gastonia Coaches* (1977), the defendant operator regularly parked eight coaches on the highway outside its offices, thereby interfering with the free passage of traffic. On the application of the Attorney General, the judge granted an injunction to restrain the defendant from causing a public nuisance by the parking of its coaches.

Similarly, in *Wandsworth LBC v Railtrack* (2002) the droppings from pigeons roosting under a railway bridge fouled the pavements and sometimes landed on passers-by. This amounted to a public nuisance. Even though Railtrack had no general control over wild pigeons, it had the necessary knowledge, opportunity and resources to have taken steps to prevent this particular nuisance, and had not done so. The council could bring an action in public nuisance, even though it had statutory powers to deal with the pigeons itself.

These cases also highlight a key distinction between public and private nuisance. In private nuisance the claimant must have a proprietary interest in the land affected. This is not a requirement of public nuisance.

Civil proceedings

The Attorney General, an individual with the consent of the Attorney General, or a local authority may bring civil proceedings in order to put an end to the nuisance.

Individual actions in tort — special damage

A public nuisance only becomes actionable at the suit of the individual, in circumstances whereby particular damage is caused to an individual over and above that suffered by the general public. The claimant in a public nuisance action has to show special damage. In *Castle v St Augustine's Links* (1922), Castle was driving his taxi when a ball driven from the defendant's golf course struck his windscreen and caused him to lose an eye. There was evidence that balls driven from this particular tee frequently landed on the highway. This case illustrates that damages for personal injury are recoverable in public nuisance.

Similarly, in *Benjamin* v *Storr* (1874) the claimant owned a coffee house in Covent Garden, adjacent to which was the defendant's auctioneer's yard. Horses used for delivering goods to the defendants often obstructed access to the claimant's shop, and the smell of their urine was very strong. The Court of Common Pleas held that the claimant had suffered direct and substantial damage over and above that suffered by the public at large, and was therefore entitled to sue in public nuisance.

Defences

Statutory authority

Many activities that interfere with the enjoyment of land are carried out by organisations operating under an Act of Parliament. Whether the defendant will be able to rely on this defence will depend on the discretion given to him/her by the Act of Parliament.

In *Metropolitan Asylum District* v *Hill* (1881), the defendants were given authority to build a smallpox hospital 'according to such plan, and in such manner, as they think fit'. The hospital was built in Hampstead and was held by the House of Lords to be a nuisance by virtue of its location. The House of Lords held that the statute merely confers a permissive power, as in this case, and that power must be exercised so as not to interfere with private rights. The defendants had the authority to build the hospital elsewhere. Similarly, in *Tate and Lyle* v *Greater London Council* (1983), the defendants were authorised by statute to design and build new ferry terminals. The defence of statutory authority partially succeeded. It was decided that some degree of siltation of the River Thames was inevitable but had the defendants taken reasonable care, the damage caused to the claimant's business by the siltation would have been reduced.

These cases can be contrasted with *Hammersmith Railway* v *Brand* (1869). The defendants had statutory authority to run trains along tracks adjoining the claimant's property. The defendants were not liable. The damaging vibration was an inevitable consequence of running the trains and an injunction would defeat the intention of the legislation. More recently, in *Allen* v *Gulf Oil Refining Ltd* (1981), the defendant company was authorised by statute to construct and operate an oil refinery. A claim in respect of the noise, smell and vibrations made by the refinery was unsuccessful, as it was an inevitable consequence.

Planning permission

It has been argued that planning permission given by a local authority is also a defence against a nuisance action, but in *Gillingham Borough Council* v *Medway (Chatham) Dock*

Co. (1993) this general argument was rejected. Here, the dock company had been given planning permission for the operation of a commercial port. Access to it was only possible via residential roads, which caused considerable traffic noise, and the council sued in public nuisance. The court held that this fact that planning permission had been granted for a particular activity did not mean that this activity could not give rise to liability in nuisance. However, the existence of planning permission could mean that the character of the neighbourhood had changed (from residential to commercial), and what might formerly have amounted to a nuisance could now be considered reasonable. The court held that this was what had happened, therefore the dock company was not liable.

Prescription

The nuisance may be legalised by the claimant's tolerating the activity for more than 20 years without complaint. However, time does not begin to run until the interference reaches a sufficient degree of severity to constitute a nuisance.

In *Sturges* v *Bridgman* (1879), the defendant had used a pestle and mortar on his premises for over 20 years. The claimant built a consulting room at the end of his garden, adjacent to the defendant's premises, and at this point the noise and vibration from the defendant's activity became unacceptable. The defendant was unable to use the defence of prescription, as the nuisance had not existed until the consulting room was built and he was consequently held liable.

This defence is available in private nuisance but not in public nuisance.

Volenti non fit injuria

The defence of *volenti non fit injuria* applies when the claimant has expressly or impliedly consented to the nuisance.

Assumption of risk

The tenant of part of premises is deemed to accept the risk of nuisance arising from the condition of any part retained by the landlord.

In *Kiddle* v *City Business Properties Ltd* (1942), the claimant leased part of the defendant's premises. A gutter on the part of the premises retained by the defendant flooded and discharged water into the claimant's shop. There was no liability as the claimant had assumed the risk.

Contributory negligence

The **Law Reform (Contributory Negligence) Act 1945** provides that the claimant's damages will be reduced according to his/her responsibility for the damage he/she has suffered.

Concealed, hidden unobservable defects in property

If the defendant can be shown to have been aware of the defect, this defence will fail. In *Leakey* v *National Trust* (1980), the surface of a hill on the defendant's land was liable to crack and debris had occasionally fallen onto the claimant's land. During the hot summer of 1976, the defendant was asked to attend to the danger but failed to do so. A large landslip subsequently damaged the claimant's property. The claimant's action in nuisance succeeded as the defendant was aware of the danger.

Act of a third party

This defence will fail if the defendant can be proven to have been aware of the danger. In *Sedleigh-Denfield* v *O'Callaghan* (1940) a trespasser on the defendant's land put a pipe in a ditch. Three years later it became blocked, causing the claimant's garden to flood. The defendant was presumed to be aware of the danger as his employees cleaned the ditch twice a year, and so was held liable.

Ineffectual defences

The activity is for the public benefit

The defendant cannot argue as a defence that his/her activity is beneficial to the public.

In *Bellew* v *Cement Co Ltd* (1948), the dust and noise from a cement factory was held to be a nuisance. An injunction was granted, despite the fact that this meant closing the only cement factory in Ireland at a time when there was an urgent public need for building new homes.

Similarly, in *Adams* v *Ursell* (1913) the defendant's fish and chip shop was situated in a residential street. The residents complained that the smell from the shop interfered with their enjoyment of their homes. The nuisance action was successful. An injunction was granted to prevent the defendant continuing his business on the premises, in spite of the argument that the shop was of great benefit to the poorer residents who lived nearby and that closing the shop would cause great hardship to the defendant.

The claimant came to the nuisance

The defendant cannot argue as a defence that he/she was carrying on his/her activity before the claimant moved nearby. In *Miller* v *Jackson* (1977), a housing estate was built next to a cricket ground. The claimants bought a house on the boundary of the cricket ground. They brought a successful nuisance action and were awarded damages in respect of the damage to property and interference caused by balls flying into their garden. The defendants' argument that cricket had been played on the ground for many years before the estate was built was no defence.

The defendant took all reasonable care to avoid the nuisance

Lindley LJ commented in *Rapier* v *London Tramways Co* (1893): 'If I am sued for nuisance, and nuisance is proved, it is no defence to say and to prove that I have taken all reasonable care to prevent it.' More recently, in *Cambridge Water Co Ltd* v *Eastern Counties Leather plc* (1994), Lord Goff stated: 'The fact that the defendant has taken all reasonable care will not of itself exonerate him.'

The rule in *Rylands* v *Fletcher*

The rule in *Rylands* v *Fletcher* was established when the case was heard in the Court of Exchequer Chamber in 1866. The facts of the case were that the defendants engaged a reputable firm of engineers to construct a reservoir on their land. Unknown to the defendants or their contractors, mineshafts under the defendants' land connected to the plaintiff's nearby coal mine. When the reservoir was filled, water poured down the shafts and flooded the plaintiff's mine.

Blackburn J formulated the rule in the following terms:

> The person who, for his own purposes, brings on his land, and collects and keeps there anything likely to do mischief if it escapes, must keep it in at his peril, and if he does not do so, is *prima facie* answerable for all the damage which is the natural consequence of its escape.

The rule requires the plaintiff to establish:
- a non-natural use of the land
- an escape of the thing brought on to the land
- damage caused by the escape
- the damage suffered is of a foreseeable type

Non-natural use

In his statement, Blackburn J makes clear that the rule applies where the defendant 'has brought something on his own property which was not naturally there'. This aspect of the rule was more fully explained by Lord Cairns when the case was appealed to the House of Lords. Therefore, a non-natural use may be 'that which in its natural condition was not in or upon it', or, alternatively, the use may be non-natural due to quantity or volume. In *Rylands* v *Fletcher* (1866), the bringing of water onto the land in quantities sufficient to fill a reservoir was held to be a non-natural use.

Subsequent case law indicates that there is no set principle on which it can be determined whether the use is non-natural, despite judicial attempts to formulate such a principle.

In *Rickards* v *Lothian* (1913), the Privy Council commented that a water supply to a lavatory was a necessary feature of town life and therefore a natural use. Lord Moulton commented that a water supply is 'in the interests of the community'. These words have since been subjected to judicial scrutiny. In *British Celanese Ltd* v *A. H. Hunt (Capacitors) Ltd,* the defendants stored metal strips on their land. In deciding that this constituted a natural use, Lawton J, approving the 'in the interests of the community' test, commented that the metal foil was there for use in the manufacture of goods that were needed for the general benefit of the community.

The expansion of what courts considered to be 'in the interests of the community', was, however, halted by the House of Lords in *Cambridge Water Co*, where the defendants operated a tannery and used a chlorinated solvent to degrease the pelts. The solvent seeped through the floor, and then through soil and layers of rock and ultimately drained into the plaintiff's bore hole situated just over a mile away. Consequently, the water, which was destined for domestic use, became unfit for human consumption. The case was decided on the issue of foreseeability of damage. However, Lord Goff commented that, despite the fact that the chemicals were commonly used in the tanning industry and that the small industrial community was worthy of support, the storage of substantial quantities of chemicals should be regarded as an almost classic case of non-natural use.

Escape

There must be an escape from the defendant's land of the thing brought onto the land. The leading case on the requirement of an escape is *Read* v *Lyons and Co Ltd* (1946). In this case, the House of Lords held that the plaintiff's action must fail as there had been no escape of the exploding shell from the defendant's land. Viscount Simon explained that there must be an escape from a place that the defendant has occupation of, or control over, to a place that is outside his/her occupation or control. Similarly, in *Ponting* v *Noakes* (1894), there was no escape. A horse was poisoned when it reached over onto the the defendant's land and ate leaves from a yew tree. The poisonous leaves had not escaped from the defendant's land. However, in *Hale* v *Jennings Bros* (1938), a tenant of a stall at a fair suffered personal injuries as the result of an escape of the defendant's chair-o-plane. It was held that this escape from one place of entertainment at a fairground to another was sufficient.

Damage caused by the escape

When he formulated the rule in *Rylands* v *Fletcher*, Blackburn J said that the defendant would be liable 'for all the damage which is the natural consequence of its escape'. Blackburn J envisaged the rule applying to all types of damage.

The case of *Rylands* v *Fletcher* itself illustrates that the rule applies to damage to land. The rule has also been held to apply to damage to chattels. In *Jones* v *Festiniog Rly Co* (1868), Blackburn J allowed the plaintiff's action to succeed when sparks from a railway engine set fire to his haystack.

Economic loss would also appear to fall within the rule, so long as it is direct. In *Weller and Co* v *Foot and Mouth Disease Research Institute* (1966), the claimant, a cattle auctioneer, did not succeed when the escape of a virus caused a loss of profit to his business after making a third party's cattle unsaleable. The auctioneer's loss of profit was contingent upon the cattle owner's loss and was therefore indirect. However, in *Ryeford Homes* v *Sevenoaks District Council* (1989), Judge Newey QC was of the opinion that economic loss was recoverable under the rule in *Rylands* v *Fletcher* when it was 'a sufficiently direct result of an escape of water from sewers'. The plaintiff in this case failed as the defence of statutory authority was successful.

Since the second half of the twentieth century, the courts have decided that the rule does not apply to personal injury. In *Transco* v *Stockport MBC* (2003), Lord Hoffman referred to *Cambridge Water Company* v *Eastern Counties Leather plc*, in which the House of Lords stated that the rule in *Rylands* v *Fletcher* was a special form of nuisance and concluded that personal injury was therefore not recoverable, as the rule is a tort against land.

The damage must be of a foreseeable type

In formulating the rule in *Rylands* v *Fletcher*, Blackburn J stated that the defendant should 'answer for the natural and anticipated consequences'. These words indicate that liability is dependant upon the damage being foreseeable. This issue was clarified in *Cambridge Water Company*. The House of Lords held that the defendants were not liable on the basis that the harm caused to the claimant's water supply was unforeseeable. Lord Goff stated: 'Foreseeability of damage of the relevant type should be regarded as a prerequisite of liability.'

Who may sue?

Throughout most of the twentieth century, the courts were of the view that a claimant did not need to have a proprietary interest in the land. In *British Celanese Ltd,* Lawton J commented: 'Once there had been an escape in this sense, those damnified may claim. They need not be the occupiers of adjoining land or indeed of any land.'

However, the position on this issue appears to have changed. In *Hunter* v *Canary Wharf*, the House of Lords held that a claimant in the tort of nuisance must have a proprietary interest in the land affected. In *Cambridge Water Company*, Lord Goff expressed the view that the rule in *Rylands* v *Fletcher* was an extension of the law of nuisance. The combination of these decisions leads to the conclusion that a proprietary interest in the land affected is now required by the claimant. This conclusion was supported by Neuberger J in *McKenna* v *British Aluminium* (2002).

Who may be sued?

In Blackburn J's original formulation of the rule, the person who will be sued is the person who accumulates the particular thing that escapes. Subsequent case law seems to indicate that occupancy, as well as ownership of the land, falls within the rule. Lord Macmillan in *Read v Lyons* specifically stated that the rule in *Rylands* v *Fletcher* was 'a principle applicable between occupiers in respect of their land'.

Specific defences

Act of third parties

This defence will not be available where the defendant ought reasonably to foresee the action of the third party and take steps to prevent it. In this respect it is useful to compare *Hale* v *Jennings Bros,* where the escape of the chair-o-plane was caused by a passenger tampering with it, with *Rickards* v *Lothian*, where the escape of water was due to a water tap on the defendant's premises being turned on by an unknown third party. In the former case the defence did not apply, whereas in the latter it did.

Act of God

This defence will apply where the escape is brought about by natural causes against which no human foresight could have guarded. The defence was successful in *Nichols* v *Marsland* (1876). The defendant had three artificial lakes on his land. Four bridges on the claimant's land were destroyed by flooding when the banks of the lakes burst during a violent thunderstorm. However, it is only in rare circumstances that the defence will be successful. In *Greenock Corporation* v *Caledonian Railway Co* (1917), unprecedented rainfall was held not to be an act of God. Lord Finlay LC said: 'Floods of extraordinary violence must be anticipated as likely to take place from time to time.'

Statutory authority

The success of this defence depends on whether the authority is obligatory or discretionary. In *Green* v *Chelsea Waterworks Co* (1894), the claimant's premises were flooded when the defendants' water main burst. The defendants were not liable. They were obliged by statute to keep the water main charged at high pressure and it was inevitable that such damage would be caused by occasional bursts.

Default of the claimant

This defence applies where the damage is due to the act or default of the claimant. In *Ponting* v *Noakes* (1894), the claimant was unsuccessful when her horse stretched over to the defendant's land and ate poisonous leaves. Not only was there no escape, but the damage was caused by the actions of the claimant's horse.

Contributory negligence

Under the **Law Reform (Contributory Negligence) Act 1945**, damages are reduced according to the claimant's responsibility for the damage suffered.

Consent of the claimant

This defence applies where the claimant expressly or impliedly consents to the accumulation of the particular thing on the defendant's land. In *Peters* v *Prince of Wales*

Theatre (Birmingham) Ltd (1943), the claimant leased his shop from the defendant. The shop was flooded when the sprinkler system burst in the adjoining theatre, also belonging to the defendant. The claimant was held to have impliedly consented to the existence of the sprinkler system, which was present at the commencement of his lease.

Vicarious liability

Vicarious liability is not an individual tort. It is a principle under which liability is imposed on a party in respect of torts (or crimes) committed by others. It arises most often in employment relationships.

There are two key requirements for the imposition of vicarious liability on the employer, these being that the tort (or crime) must (a) be committed by an employee, and (b) be committed in the course of his/her employment.

Who is an employee?

There is no single set test for the courts to apply in deciding whether the wrongdoer is an employee. This is due to the broad range of employment relationships that exists, and the shortcomings of the tests developed so far by the courts.

The control test

The control test was the first attempt by the courts to establish a mechanism by which they could decide whether the wrongdoer was an employee. In *Collins* v *Hertfordshire County Council* (1947), Hilbery J explained that as the worker was an employee, the employer 'cannot only order or require what is to be done but how it shall be done'. In this case, the defendant was not liable for the negligence of a surgeon, which resulted in the death of a patient, because Hilbery J concluded that the council could not control in any way how the surgeon was to perform his duties.

The inadequacy of the control test as the sole determining factor was recognised by Lord Thankerton in *Short* v *J. W. Henderson Ltd* (1946). He suggested further key features of an employment relationship including the power to select, suspend and dismiss, the power to control the method of working, and the payment of wages.

The decision of Hilbery J was much criticised in *Cassidy* v *Ministry of Health* (1951). A patient suffered permanent injury to his hand, allegedly through the negligence of the surgeon performing the operation. The surgeon was held to be the employee of the hospital authority. Lord Denning explained that the determining factor of whether the worker was an employee was not that the employer controlled the method of work, but rather that the employer had the power to select and dismiss.

The control test nevertheless remains useful as a determining factor in some circumstances, for example when employees are hired out to work for others. In *Mersey Docks*

Harbour Board v *Coggins and Griffith* (1946), a harbour board hired out a crane and driver to the claimant under a contract, making the driver the servant of the claimant. When an accident occurred through the driver's negligence, the court held he was still effectively the servant of the harbour board. The harbour board was responsible for paying the driver and retained the power of dismissal. It also controlled the way the driver operated the crane. However, in *Viasystems* v *Thermal Transfer* (2005) the Court of Appeal ruled that in such 'shared employment' cases the correct approach (per May LJ) was to decide in respect of each employer separately whether it had the power to control the actions of the employee, but there was no reason why, if both employers could direct the employee, they should not be jointly liable.

The economic reality or multiple test

This test recognises that a single test of employment is not satisfactory and was developed by McKenna J in *Ready Mixed Concrete* v *MPNI* (1968). A contract between the defendant firm and its driver provided for the driver to own his own lorry (bought with money loaned by an associate finance company). It was the responsibility of the driver to maintain the lorry and to do whatever was needed to make the lorry and a driver available throughout the contract period. McKenna J said factors to be considered when determining the existence of a contract of employment include:

- whether there is payment of a wage
- whether tools for the job are provided by the employer or the worker
- whether the worker has to obey orders
- the exercise of control over the way the work is done
- the acceptance of the business risk

No one factor is by itself conclusive. McKenna J stipulated three conditions that must be met before an employment relationship is identified:

(1) The employee agrees in return for a wage or other remuneration that he/she will provide his/her work and skill for the employer.

(2) The employee agrees expressly or impliedly to be subject to the employer's control.

(3) The other terms of the contract are consistent with there being a contract of employment.

In this case, the claimant driver had taken a certain business risk himself and so was held to be an independent contractor and not an employee.

The economic reality test has since been modified, so that all factors in the relationship should be considered and weighed according to their significance. Relevant factors, in addition to those mentioned above, include the method of payment, tax and National Insurance (NI) contributions and self-description.

In some workplace situations, the parties may have decided the status of the employment relationship for themselves. The most usual reasons for having a contract for services, whereby the worker is self-employed, as opposed to a contract of service giving the worker employee status, are to avoid tax deductions under the PAYE system and to take advantage of a more favourable level of NI contributions. From the view of the employer, the advantage of hiring a worker on a self-employed basis is that the worker does not have the extensive provision of statutory employment rights afforded to employees, for example, the right to redundancy pay. A case illustrating the inconclusiveness of the parties' description of their working relationship is *Ferguson* v *John Dawson Ltd* (1976). The claimant worked as a self-employed labourer on a building site. This meant that the claimant paid less income tax. When the claimant was injured as a result of falling off the roof, the defendants argued that their duty to provide a guardrail was only owed to employees. The court held that, despite the self-description of the working relationship, the claimant was, in reality, an employee. The defendants controlled what work was done, and how and when the claimant did it.

The course of employment

The employer will only be held vicariously liable for the torts (crimes) of the employee if at the time of the wrongdoing the employee was acting in the course of his/her employment.

There are no set criteria for determining what amounts to the course of employment; however, it is useful to consider the categories of circumstances which the courts have held to fall inside or outside its scope.

Authorised acts carried out in an unauthorised manner

Broadly speaking, this category of acts is concerned with circumstances where the employee is doing what he/she is employed to do but in a manner that has not been authorised by the employer. There are many different means by which an act may be unauthorised.

In some situations the act may be carried out in an unauthorised way because the employee has acted overzealously in order to protect the property of the employer. In *Vasey* v *Surrey Free Inns* (1996), the claimant was refused entry to a club by two doormen who were employees of the defendant. In a temper, the claimant kicked and damaged a glass window before walking away. The doormen chased the claimant across the car park and assaulted him with a cosh. The Court of Appeal held that the employer was vicariously liable for the assault. The doormen were doing their job, i.e. using force to protect their employer's property, but did so in an excessive way.

However, where the employee, while at work, uses violence to settle a personal dispute, the courts will hold his/her actions to be beyond the scope of his/her employment. In *Warren* v *Henlys* (1948), a garage attendant used violent language in wrongly accusing a driver of trying to leave the garage without paying. After paying, the driver told the garage attendant he would report him to his employers. The garage attendant punched the driver in the face. The driver claimed damages, but the garage owners were not held to be vicariously liable. The actions of the garage attendant were of personal vengeance, not an unauthorised way of performing his job, and so were outside the course of employment.

An act may be conducted in an impliedly unauthorised way because the employer would have so prohibited it had he/she thought about it. In *Century Insurance* v *Northern Ireland Road Transport* (1942), an employee driver of petrol tankers was delivering petrol to a garage. While the petrol was being transferred into the tankers he lit a cigarette and negligently threw away the lighted match, causing an explosion and extensive damage. The House of Lords held that the driver was acting in the course of his employment. Part of his job was to wait while the petrol was transferred. Although lighting the cigarette was for his own benefit, this was not enough to relieve his employers of their liability.

Sometimes the employee will perform an unauthorised act in a manner expressly prohibited by the employer. Provided the employee is doing acts he/she is employed to do, the employer will be held vicariously liable. In *Limpus* v *London Omnibus* (1862), the drivers of horse-drawn buses were expressly forbidden to race their buses, a practice engaged in by rival bus drivers in order to get custom. One driver did so and caused an accident. The company was held to be vicariously liable. The driver was doing what he was authorised to do, driving the bus, but was doing so in an expressly unauthorised manner. This case can be compared to *Iqbal* v *London Transport Executive* (1973). A bus conductor, trying to be helpful, drove a bus, despite having been specifically forbidden to do so. His negligent driving caused damage, but the employers were held not to be vicariously liable. The act of driving the bus was not an act the conductor was employed to do — he was employed to collect fares.

Rose v *Plenty* (1976) is another decision illustrating the courts' approach to expressly prohibited modes of performing employment duties. A milkman, against orders to the contrary, allowed a 13-year-old boy to help him on his round. The boy was injured as a result of the milkman's negligent driving. The Court of Appeal held the dairy to be vicariously liable. The milkman was doing what he was employed to do, i.e. deliver milk, but was doing so in an expressly unauthorised way.

Activities outside normal hours of work

The course of employment includes not only activities carried out during normal hours of work but also activities that are closely connected.

In *Ruddiman and Co* v *Smith* (1889), an employee went to wash his hands a few minutes after his working day ended. He left the tap running and the resulting overflow damaged the claimant's adjoining premises. The court held that the negligent act was incidental to the employment and accordingly the employers were vicariously liable.

Collecting one's wages at the end of the working day has also been held to be within the course of employment. In *Staton* v *National Coal Board* (1957), the claimant's husband was killed by the defendant's negligent employee who, having completed his work for the day, was on his way to collect his wages. The defendant was held vicariously liable.

Activities of an employee while off the employer's premises may also be sufficiently related to his/her employment to fall within the principle. In *Weir* v *Chief Constable of Merseyside Police* (2003), an off-duty police officer was held to be acting in the course of employment when he assaulted the claimant and manhandled him down some stairs and into a police van following an argument about personal matters. The officer had identified himself to the claimant as a police officer and had acted as one, albeit very badly, and that was sufficient.

Liability for employee's torts committed while travelling to and from work

The general position is that most journeys to and from work are outside the course of employment. However, journeys where the employee is being paid for the time during which he/she is travelling, and for which he/she is receiving travel expenses, may be within the course of employment. In *Smith* v *Stages* (1989), an employee was injured while travelling home due to another employee's negligent driving. The employees had worked 24 hours without a break and decided to drive straight back, having had no sleep. The House of Lords held the employer to be vicariously liable because the employees were paid wages to cover the journey time.

Discrimination

A more generous approach to what constitutes the 'course of employment' is adopted by the courts in circumstances where anti-discrimination legislation applies. In *Jones* v *Tower Boot Company* (1997), a young black worker was subjected to racist taunts and physical abuse by workmates. The employment appeal tribunal held the actions of the employees to be outside the scope of their employment. The Court of Appeal, reversing the decision of the employment appeal tribunal, held that the **Race Discrimination Act 1976** made the employer liable for all discriminatory acts committed by employees in the course of their employment. The employer was therefore vicariously liable.

Situations where the employee is outside the scope of employment

The employer will not be vicariously liable for activities performed by the employee that have no relevance to the job he/she is employed to do. In these circumstances, the employee is said to be 'on a frolic of his own'.

In *General Engineering Services* v *Kingston and Saint Andrew Corporation* (1988), firemen working a 'go-slow' in support of a pay claim took 17 minutes to complete a journey of three and a half minutes. By the time the firemen arrived at the fire, the claimant's factory had been completely destroyed. The Privy Council held that the employers were not vicariously liable for the damage. The firemen's action was not an unauthorised way of doing their job, but was tantamount to a refusal to do their job at all.

A similar approach was taken by the Court of Appeal in *Heasmans* v *Clarity Cleaning* (1987). The defendants were contracted to clean the claimant's offices. A cleaner employed by the defendants used the claimant's telephones to make a number of long distance calls costing approximately £1,400. The defendants were not vicariously liable. While the cleaner's employment had put him in the position to make the calls, it was a wholly unauthorised act and therefore not in the course of his employment.

When employees who travel from place to place as part of their job take a detour for their own benefit they will be acting outside the course of employment. In *Storey* v

Ashton (1869), a wine merchant's driver and clerk went out to deliver some wine and collect empty bottles. On the way back, they took a detour in order to fetch a cask belonging to the clerk, and ran over the claimant. The claimant sued for damages. The court held that the employer was not vicariously liable. The driver was not on his employer's business at the time of the accident, but on 'a frolic of his own'. This case is easily distinguishable from *Smith* v *Stages* in which the employees had clearly been on the employer's business.

An evaluation of vicarious liability

Candidates who wish to prepare for an exam question requiring evaluation of vicarious liability may find it useful to develop the following points:

- Application of the vicarious liability principle will often result in the injustice that someone who is not at fault is held liable. This is contrary to the general principle of English law that there should be no liability without fault.
- The law is not precisely clear on the definition of an employee. This is partly due to there being so many different employment relationships. Although case law has clarified the position with regard to some workers, e.g. doctors (*Cassidy* v *Ministry of Health*, 1951), with other relationships the position remains unclear. This is the case with outworkers (people who work from home), although if they are doing the same work as those in the workplace they will be classed as employees (*Nethermere (St Neots) Ltd* v *Taverna and Gardiner*, 1984).
- All tests for determining who is an employee, including the economic reality test as now used, are open to interpretation. As yet there is no absolute or definitive test.
- Many workers fall outside the status of employee, e.g. apprentices and agency workers. There is no one to pay for the result of the tortious activities of such workers. Victims are therefore not compensated.

However, there are many justifications for the imposition of such liability. These include:

- The purpose of employment is to allow the employer to profit from the employee's work.
- The employee may have committed the tort on the employer's behalf.
- An employer may have a degree of control over his/her employees. The employer has the ultimate power of dismissal and should therefore be able to ensure that his/her employees do not perform their work in a careless way.
- The injured party needs to sue someone who is able to afford to pay damages. In this respect, the employer is more easily identifiable than the particular employee at fault, and is more likely to be in a position to pay damages, not least by virtue of the obligation to take out public liability insurance. Furthermore, the employer can more easily pass on loss, for example by raising prices.

General defences

Throughout this guide, the defences specific to particular torts have been considered in context. There are, however, general defences that are applicable to most torts. The AQA specification requires candidates to consider the general defences of contributory negligence and *volenti non fit injuria*.

Contributory negligence

Until 1945, contributory negligence was a complete defence. A negligent defendant could avoid paying any compensation if he/she could show that the victim had in some way contributed to his/her loss. The injustice caused to such victims prompted Parliament to remedy the situation by passing the **Law Reform (Contributory Negligence) Act 1945**. Section 1(1) of the 1945 Act provides:

> Where any person suffers damage as the result of his own fault and partly of the fault of any other person or persons, a claim in respect of that damage shall not be defeated by reason of the fault of the person suffering the damage, but the damages recoverable in respect thereof shall be reduced to such extent as the court thinks just and equitable having regard to the claimant's share in the responsibility for the damage.

The effect of the 1945 Act is that contributory negligence is a partial defence which, if proved, results in the claimant's damages being reduced according to his/her responsibility for the loss suffered. While the wording of s.1 appears to be clear on this issue, there has nevertheless been uncertainty in the Court of Appeal on the question of whether damages can be reduced by 100%. In *Jayes* v *IMI Kynock* (1985), the claimant was injured while checking an unfenced machine. He succeeded in an action for statutory duty, as the machine should have been fenced. The Court of Appeal upheld the decision of the first-instance court and reduced damages by 100% due to the claimant's admission that he had behaved foolishly. However, in *Anderson* v *Newham College* (2003), the Court of Appeal disapproved its decision in *Jayes* and held that the defence of contributory negligence is only relevant in circumstances where the defendant is partly to blame. In such circumstances, damages should not be reduced by 100%. The *Anderson* case would appear to be more in line with the wording of s.1 of the 1945 Act.

The wording of s.1 is focused on the damage suffered by the claimant. It is important to consider what has caused the damage rather than merely what has caused the accident. Lord Denning in *Froom* v *Butcher* (1975) said: 'The question is not what was the cause of the accident. It is rather what was the cause of the damage.' This point is clearly illustrated by some of the road traffic accident cases in which the defence has been successfully raised. In *O'Connell* v *Jackson* (1972), a moped driver was injured while not wearing a crash helmet. Damages were reduced by 15%. In *Froom* v *Butcher* (1975), the claimant was not wearing a seat belt and was injured in an accident caused by the defendant. Damages were reduced by 25%. In none of these cases was the accident caused by the negligence of the claimants, but in each case their injuries were more serious due to the failure to take reasonable care for their own safety.

Emergencies

The requirement placed on the claimant to take reasonable care for his/her safety is important in the context of emergency situations. Therefore, any action taken by the claimant that is reasonable in the agony of the moment and results in injury to himself/herself will not amount to contributory negligence. In *Jones* v *Boyce* (1816), the claimant jumped from a coach and broke his leg after he saw that the coach was in imminent danger of overturning due to the breaking of a coupling rein. The coach was then halted safely. The court held that the claimant had acted reasonably in the agony of the moment and could therefore recover damages in full.

Children

There is no clear indication in the 1945 Act as to the age at which children can be guilty of contributory negligence. However, while no set guidelines on specific age limits can be gleaned from the case law, the decisions do give some indication of future outcomes. For example, in *Snelling* v *Whitehead* (1975), the House of Lords was clear that contributory negligence would have been an irrelevant factor as the claimant was only 7 years old. In *Morales* v *Eccleston* (1991), the Court of Appeal held the 11-year-old claimant to be 75% responsible for his injuries. He had run out into a road without looking and was struck by a car. His damages were reduced by 75% accordingly. In *Gough* v *Thorne* (1966), Lord Denning, taking a more lenient approach, held that the 13-year-old claimant was not guilty of contributory negligence on similar facts, on the basis that a child does not have the same road sense as an adult.

Volenti non fit injuria

The Latin maxim *volenti non fit injuria* is usually expressed as 'voluntary assumption of risk'. Unlike contributory negligence, *volenti non fit injuria* is a complete defence which, if established, will result in the victim receiving no compensation. The essential elements of *volenti non fit injuria* are that the victim:
- knows of the risk
- voluntarily decides to take the risk of injury, and
- expressly or impliedly agrees to waive any claim in respect of such injury

Knowledge of the risk

A person cannot be *volenti* to a risk of which he/she has no knowledge. This is the case even if it can be shown that the reasonable person would have been aware of the risk. In *Murray* v *Harringay Arena* (1951), a 6-year-old spectator was injured when an ice-hockey puck was struck out of the rink. Due to the likelihood of the risk, the claim against the organisers failed on the basis that there was no breach of duty. However, the Court of Appeal commented that a 6-year-old could not be attributed with knowledge of the risk and the defence of *volenti* was, therefore, irrelevant to the case.

The requirement of knowledge is also illustrated by the more recent case of *Vine* v *Waltham Forest LBC* (2000). The claimant had become ill while out driving and needed to vomit. She left her car in a private car park for a short while and returned to find it clamped. The defence did not apply because the claimant had no knowledge of the risk of the car being clamped. In her distressed condition, she had not seen the warning notices.

Mere knowledge of the risk does not constitute consent

It is important to note the distinction between knowledge and consent. It cannot necessarily be said that a person consents to a risk of injury merely because he/she is aware of it. This aspect of the defence was emphasised by the House of Lords in *Smith* v *Baker* (1891). The claimant and other employees were aware that a crane often swung heavy stones above them as they worked, although no warning was given to the employees of particular times when the crane would be operating. The claimant was injured when a stone from the crane fell on him. The House of Lords held that the defence of *volenti* did not apply. Lord Herschell said mere continuance in service with knowledge of the risk did not constitute consent.

Consent must be given voluntarily

Voluntary consent requires a person to be in a position to choose freely. He/she must have full knowledge of the relevant circumstances, and there must be an absence of any constraints that might interfere with freedom of will.

In *Morris* v *Murray* (1990), the claimant was a passenger in a light aircraft being flown by his friend. Both the men had been drinking heavily for many hours before they boarded the plane. It was estimated that the pilot had consumed 17 whiskies. The aircraft crashed, killing the pilot and seriously injuring the claimant. The defence of *volenti* was successful. The claimant had knowingly and willingly embarked on a flight with a drunken pilot and there had been no compulsion to do so.

It is clear that in the workplace the employee's perception of the likely effect on employment prospects may constitute a feeling of constraint that interferes with his/her freedom of choice. One case in which there was said to be no such interference was *Imperial Chemical Industries Ltd* v *Shatwell* (1965). The claimant and his brother were shot firers employed by the defendants. They decided to test a circuit of detonators, ignoring the employer's usual safety procedures and warnings, and were both injured. The dangers of not taking precautions had been highlighted to the employees by the employers, and employees who continued to disobey instructions had been sacked. The House of Lords allowed the defence of *volenti* to succeed. The defence is also likely to succeed where the claimant is employed to do work that necessarily involves danger. In *Bowater* v *Rowley Regis Corp* (1944), Goddard LJ gave, as an example, working in an explosives factory where there would always be a risk of an explosion even when all statutory provisions and procedural safeguards were observed.

A further category of cases in which the claimant may be said to voluntarily assume the risk of injury is sporting cases. The principle applied by the courts is that the claimant, whether a spectator or a participant, only consents to the risks ordinarily incidental to the particular sport. In *Wooldridge* v *Sumner* (1963), the claimant, a photographer, was struck by a horse competing at an equestrian event. The rider had, in an error of judgement, taken a corner too fast. The defence of *volenti* applied. However, in *Condon* v *Basi* (1985), the defence did not apply. The claimant sustained a broken leg as a result of a tackle by the defendant, which was said by the referee to constitute foul play. The defendant was liable on the basis that a footballer only consents to tackles that the rules of the game permit.

Rescue cases

The courts take a more sympathetic approach to rescuers. The law should not discourage people from coming to the aid of those in danger. In *Haynes* v *Harwood* (1935), a policeman was injured while attempting to stop a horse bolting along a busy street. The Court of Appeal rejected the *volenti* defence. The claimant had taken a personal risk in order to eliminate the danger to others in the street. The same approach was adopted by the Court of Appeal in *Baker* v *Hopkins* (1959) where a doctor, knowing the risk he was taking, insisted on going down a well to try to help two workmen who had been overcome by carbon monoxide fumes. The doctor was also overcome by the fumes and died. The *volenti* defence was rejected and the doctor's widow succeeded in her claim.

Remedies

The specification requires candidates to acquire outline knowledge of civil remedies. Questions will sometimes specifically ask for consideration of the remedies available to the claimant. This is particularly so with nuisance questions, which usually require a brief explanation and application of both injunctions and damages, and negligence and occupiers' liability questions, which usually require a brief explanation and application of damages.

Damages

Candidates are advised to revisit pages 33–35 in the Unit 3 guide dealing with damages. It is important that candidates are able to explain and apply the concepts of general and special damages, pecuniary and non-pecuniary losses and to consider

content guidance

how the courts calculate damages using the multiplier and multiplicand. Reference may also be made to provisional damages and structured settlements.

Injunctions

The injunction is an equitable remedy and as such is available at the discretion of the court unlike damages, which are available as a right to the successful party. The court will take into account the equitable principles such as 'let right be done' and 'he who comes to equity must come with clean hands'. When answering an exam question it is, therefore, important to recognise that the behaviour of the defendant may be relevant in this respect.

In *Christie* v *Davey* (1893), the claimant was a music teacher who gave lessons at home. This irritated the defendant, who lived in an adjoining property. He responded by banging trays on the wall, blowing whistles and shouting to disrupt the music activities. The claimant was successful in seeking an injunction. The behaviour of the defendant was malicious and unreasonable. Similarly, in *Hollywood Silver Fox Farm* the defendant attempted to interrupt the claimant's breeding of silver foxes by firing guns on his own land but close to the claimant's land. An injunction was granted due to the malice of the defendant.

An injunction is a court order and may be mandatory (ordering the defendant to do something) or prohibitory (ordering the defendant *not* to do something). Mandatory injunctions are rarely given. There must be a strong probability of grave damage to the claimant and damages must be an inadequate remedy. The likelihood of hardship to the defendant is also taken into account. Prohibitory injunctions are frequently made in cases involving trespass or nuisance, the idea being that the defendant should not be able to buy the right to commit the tort. Hardship to the defendant is not considered. You should expect to have to consider the relevance of an injunction when answering a nuisance question.

Injunctions may be sought in both public and private nuisance actions. In *Attorney General* v *PYA Quarries*, the Attorney General successfully brought an action to restrain the activity of PYA Quarries on behalf of local residents who were disturbed by vibrations and dust.

The injunction may be granted to limit the activity of the defendant rather than prevent it altogether. In *Kennaway* v *Thompson*, the claimant lived by Lake Windermere. The defendants used the lake for powerboat racing. The claimant was granted an injunction that limited the frequency of the racing and the noise level of the powerboats. This case illustrates the approach of the courts in balancing the interests of both parties when considering the injunction.

While public interest is not considered in deciding whether an activity constitutes a nuisance, the courts do consider it when determining whether the claimant should be awarded an injunction. *Miller* v *Jackson* provides further illustration of this issue. The claimants bought a house next to a cricket ground and suffered interference with enjoyment of their property and property damage caused by cricket balls escaping from the ground. The activity of the cricket club was held to constitute a nuisance but Lord Denning emphasised the public importance of playing cricket and denied the claimant an injunction. However, damages were awarded.

Questions
&
Answers

This section of the guide provides you with five questions, which cover all of the Unit 5 topics — each separate tort and any appropriate defences. Each question is followed by an A-grade answer which demonstrates both the structure that you should follow and how to use case and statutory authorities.

C-grade answers have also been included for questions 1–4 to illustrate some of the common problems that lead unnecessarily to students achieving lower marks. Note the importance of using cases effectively — failure to use cases is one of the most significant differences between A- and C-grade answers.

To acquire the necessary skills and to become more familiar with this style of examination question, it is a good idea to practise adapting the A-grade answers for different scenarios. You are strongly encouraged to download past papers and mark schemes from AQA (**www.aqa.org.uk**) or to obtain these from your teacher.

The mnemonic **IDEA** may help you to answer problem-solving questions that are based on a short scenario:

I   **Identify** all the relevant tort actions *and* possible defences.
D   **Define** the key legal elements of each of these.
E   **Explain** in detail the various legal rules.
A   **Apply** these rules to the facts of the scenario, using authorities — both cases and statutes — to support your answer.

Examiner's comments

The candidate answers are accompanied by examiner's comments, preceded by the icon ☑. These explain the elements of the answer for which marks can be awarded, and are intended to give you an insight into what examiners are looking for. For A-grade answers, the examiner's comments show why high marks would be given. The comments given for C-grade answers point out the various weaknesses — lack of cases, inadequate explanation and irrelevant material, all of which cause marks to be lost.

Psychiatric injury

Javed owned a warehouse with an open yard surrounded by a low wall. For years, the yard was little used and members of the public treated it as a short cut from a main road to a housing estate. Then Javed began to store materials in the yard and put up a light fencing and signs warning that the yard was private property. Recently, the signs have been torn down, gaps in the fencing have appeared and members of the public, including Ken, have been using the yard as a short cut again. Ken was crossing the yard while Les, an inexperienced forklift-truck driver, was trying to stack heavy crates. As Ken tried to slip through a narrow gap, the stack of crates toppled over and he was crushed and badly injured.

Mike had been assisting Les and had narrowly avoided being crushed himself. He immediately got down on the ground and tried to assist Ken. The incident was witnessed by Mike's sister, Nicola, who had come to collect him from work. She could just glimpse Mike's legs and thought that he had been crushed in the incident. She immediately became hysterical and was taken away for treatment. Mike found it difficult to recover from the experience and was off work for weeks. Nicola suffered panic attacks for the next few months.

Source: June 2003, AQA Paper 5, question 4(b)

Consider what rights Mike and Nicola may have against Javed.   (25 marks)

■ ■ ■

A-grade answer

With regard to both potential claimants — Mike and Nicola — it is necessary to examine the relevant issues concerning recovery for psychiatric injury. This is an area of tort law that has developed considerably in recent years.

The tort of negligence has experienced little difficulty in awarding damages for physical injuries or property damage resulting from negligence, or for psychiatric injury following from physical injury, but the issue of psychiatric injury in isolation has given rise to a slightly different set of rules.

There are two key issues to be addressed in all such claims. The first of these deals with the basic principles of the tort of negligence — whether the claimant was owed a duty of care by the defendant, whether in the circumstances of the case the defendant breached that duty, and finally, whether the injury was caused by the breach and was not too remote. The second issue is whether the claimant was a primary or secondary victim.

> This answer has a strong introduction, effectively providing a 'table of contents' that addresses the separate key elements of the potential content in the mark scheme.

As a fellow employee, Mike was certainly owed a duty of care by his employer, Javed, (under both the neighbour principle of foreseeable injury/loss from *Donoghue* v *Stevenson* and occupier's liability) and it also seems clear that Les, an inexperienced fork-lift truck driver, breached that duty of care when the stack of crates toppled over — the 'reasonable' forklift driver would not have caused the crates to topple, and under the test laid down in *Nettleship* v *Weston,* the test is objective and does not take into account Les's inexperience. The consequence of Mike's difficulties that caused him to be off work for weeks was not too remote from the breach — the *Wagon Mound* test — and had his injuries been physical rather than psychiatric, Mike would have had no difficulty in recovering damages. Mike has, however, found it difficult to recover from the experience, which suggests nervous shock. The legal rule is that there must be some recognisable psychiatric injury, supported by medical evidence. Ordinary human emotions, such as grief and distress, do not qualify as nervous shock. For example, in *Reilly* v *Merseyside Health Authority* the claimants could not recover damages for their worry and panic when they were trapped in a lift for over an hour. The fact that Mike was off work for weeks could well indicate that he was suffering from a diagnosable psychiatric injury.

> Although this is a nervous shock question, the basic rules of negligence still need to be dealt with, and the candidate has covered all three rules effectively — duty, breach and remoteness. The reference to *Nettleship* in breach, addressing the fact that Les was an inexperienced driver, is noteworthy. Candidates need to be able to recognise relevant cases from the facts of the scenario.

If that is indeed the case, the next issue is whether Mike is a primary or secondary victim. Primary victims are those who are directly affected by the negligent act, those who believe themselves to be in physical danger and rescuers. In the circumstances of the incident, it could be argued that Mike was a primary victim both in respect of him being a rescuer (*Chadwick* v *British Transport Commission*) and also being in the immediate vicinity of the accident and thus fearing for his own safety. He had 'narrowly avoided being crushed himself' and therefore comes within the test established in *Dulieu* v *White* where due to the driver's negligence, a horse-drawn van owned by the defendant crashed into a pub run by the claimant's husband. The claimant, who was serving behind the bar, suffered shock and gave birth prematurely. The case of *Chadwick* established the general rule that rescuers will be treated as primary victims, provided they can show close involvement with the incident, which Mike would have no difficulty proving. The House of Lords in *White* v *Chief Constable of South Yorkshire* introduced the requirement for rescuers to place themselves in danger or to perceive they are doing so when making a claim in respect of psychiatric injury. Primary victims are able to claim for psychiatric injury under the normal rules of negligence, and therefore Mike should be able to claim damages to compensate him fully for the weeks taken off work.

e The issue of whether the claimant is a primary or secondary victim is crucial in such questions, and all the various factors need to be identified and properly explained. This has been done well here, with relevant cases used to provide a sound foundation to both argument and conclusion.

The position of Nicola is much more problematic — she is clearly not a primary victim under any of the categories explained above. She would have to establish that the defendant was in breach of his duty of care towards her, and that his negligence caused her psychiatric injuries. Here, it could be argued that Javed did owe her a duty of care arising both from occupier's liability (Occupiers' Liability Act 1957) and the neighbour principle referred to above. The law governing the right of secondary victims to claim for nervous shock has been clearly laid down by the House of Lords in the leading case of *Alcock* v *Chief Constable of South Yorkshire*. Here, the conditions under which a secondary victim could successfully claim stipulate that the victim had to be present at the shocking event itself or its immediate aftermath, that he/she must have close ties of love and affection with the primary victim and that he/she must have learned of the event by his/her own unaided senses. Finally, the psychiatric injury must be induced by the sudden appreciation of the horrifying event and not develop gradually over a period of time.

In the instant case, Nicola could argue that she satisfies at least three of these requirements in that she was present at the incident and witnessed it herself, and the psychiatric injury was induced suddenly. The question clearly states, 'She immediately became hysterical and was taken away for treatment'. Furthermore, it would appear that Nicola has suffered a recognised psychiatric injury, as she has received treatment. There is, however, some difficulty with the requirement that there be close ties of love and affection with the primary victim. In *Alcock* this was restricted in general to spouses and parent-child relationships, although in that case, a fiancée was included under this heading, and it was suggested *obiter* that siblings might also be able to recover damages if they could produce sufficient evidence of such ties of love and affection.

In conclusion, therefore, it can be argued that Mike would be entitled to recover damages for his time off work as a primary victim, and that Nicola, provided she could satisfy the test of close love and affection, would also be able to recover damages as a secondary victim.

e Although the issues of duty, breach and remoteness could have been covered more fully, the issue of Nicola being a secondary victim is fully explained. *Alcock* is the key case for this, and a sound answer requires all three tests to be addressed, as has been done here. The reference to the *obiter* statement on the question of siblings is very useful in confirming the depth of understanding of this particular rule.

Overall, this answer is sound on negligence rules, and primary and secondary victims; all key cases are used effectively and there is sound application. It would receive the full 25 marks.

C-grade answer

Mike and Nicola may both have a claim against Javed if they can prove they have suffered psychiatric injury. Mike has been off work for weeks because he has found it difficult to recover from the experience and Nicola has suffered panic attacks for months.

When claimants bring an action against the defendant in respect of psychiatric injury, the action will only be successful if it is proved that the psychiatric injury is medically recognised. Grief and other normal psychological reactions to accidents do not constitute psychiatric injury. In the scenario it states that Nicola has had treatment, which would indicate that her condition is medically recognised. Mike has been off work for weeks because he cannot recover from the experience, which would also indicate a long-term recognisable condition.

The courts have established that there are different categories of claimant in respect of psychiatric injury claims. Primary victims are people who are directly involved in the accident and suffer psychiatric injury as a result of fearing for their own safety. Secondary victims are people who are not directly involved in the accident but suffer psychiatric injury as a result of fearing for the safety of those people who are involved. The law also allows claims from rescuers, provided they have placed themselves in danger in effecting the rescue or perceived that they were doing so.

In this scenario, Mike could bring a claim as a primary victim as he is involved in the accident. He had narrowly avoided being crushed himself. He could also possibly bring a claim as a rescuer, provided he could satisfy the requirement that he placed himself in danger or perceived he was doing so while assisting Ken, who was under a stack of crates.

Nicola however, would have to bring a claim as a secondary victim as she was not directly involved in the accident. Following the decision in *Alcock* v *Chief Constable of South Yorkshire*, those who bring an action as secondary victims have to satisfy certain criteria. First, the secondary victim must have been present at the scene and witnessed the accident with his/her unaided senses or must have come upon the immediate aftermath. In this case, Nicola has come upon the immediate aftermath. Second, the secondary victim must have close ties of love and affection with the primary victim. In this case, the relationship in question is between a brother and a sister. It is possible that Nicola might be able to satisfy this requirement but she will have to specifically prove her close ties with Mike. Third, the secondary victim must suffer the psychiatric injury suddenly. Nicola would satisfy this requirement as she immediately became hysterical and was taken away for treatment.

In conclusion, Mike would be able to claim as a primary victim and Nicola would be able to claim as a secondary victim, provided she could satisfy the court that she had close ties of love and affection with Mike.

e While this answer deals quite well with explanation and application of the law relating to primary and secondary victims claiming for psychiatric injury, there is a lack of authority throughout. *Alcock* is correctly considered, but further relevant case law is required for a more sound argument. This answer also omits to mention that psychiatric injury is a special duty situation and that any action by Mike or Nicola will be based in negligence. Consequently, there is no consideration of the relevant aspects of duty, breach and causation. As with questions relating to economic loss, this is a common omission of weaker candidates. The answer would be awarded 14 or 15 marks.

uestion 2

Pure economic loss and negligent misstatement

An article in the IT pages of the *Herald*, a national newspaper, described and recommended Safestore, a security software package. After reading the article, Gordon bought a copy of Safestore and installed it on his computer's hard disk, hoping to protect his clients' confidential business information. In fact, the article had failed to explain that the version of Safestore on public sale was less comprehensive than the version reviewed. Gordon's security was breached 2 months later while he was online. In consequence, he had to pay a total of £30,000 to clients affected by the breach and he stopped receiving orders for his services. Gordon has now discovered that the manufacturer of Safestore has ceased to trade.

Source: January 2004, AQA Paper 5, question 3(a)

Consider what rights Gordon may have against the *Herald* in connection with the £30,000 he had to pay out and his loss of business.   (25 marks)

■ ■ ■

A-grade answer

In order to answer the question as to whether Gordon has any rights against the *Herald* newspaper in respect of his £30,000 loss, it is first necessary to consider the basic rules of the tort of negligence. The first major issue is whether or not in the circumstances the *Herald* owes Gordon a duty of care. The tests used to establish this are the neighbour test from *Donoghue* v *Stevenson*, which relies on the question of foreseeability of harm or loss, and the more modern incremental approach from *Caparo* v *Dickman* which requires two further issues to be examined — proximity and policy.

In the instant case, it can certainly be argued that it was foreseeable that as a result of the negligently written article in the *Herald*, a reader could suffer financial losses. However, the mere reading of a national newspaper is not by itself sufficient to establish proximity — closeness in terms of time, space or relationship. A further problem for Gordon is the policy test — whether it is just, fair and reasonable to impose a duty of care. This issue was considered in *Caparo* where it was held by the House of Lords that a duty of care was not owed by the auditors to shareholders. Lord Bridge specifically addressed the question of recovery for pure economic loss when he stated: 'One of the most important distinctions lies in the law's essentially different approach to the different kinds of damage. It is one thing to owe a duty of care to avoid causing injury to the person or property of another; it is quite another to avoid causing others to suffer purely economic loss.'

🖉 Referring to the basic rules of duty of care within the tort of negligence is the best way to start this answer. Too often candidates make the serious error of ignoring negligence rules, which form the basis of recovery of economic loss problems. Effective use is made of the *Caparo* rules, especially the rule of proximity.

The courts have decided that pure economic loss is not generally recoverable unless it is the direct result of injury to the claimant or damage to his/her property, as in *Mulvaine* v *Joseph* where a professional golfer was awarded an additional £1,000 for the loss of future prize money after he was injured in a road accident. Pure economic loss may also be recovered if it arises from a negligent misstatement made by the defendant to the claimant, provided there was a 'special relationship' between them when the misstatement was made. This rule was laid down in *Heller* v *Hedley Byrne*. In that case, Lord Devlin defined the nature of the special relationship as 'a responsibility that is voluntarily undertaken, either where there is a general relationship such as that of solicitor and client, or specifically in relation to a particular transaction'. Clearly, in this case, there can be no possibility of any general relationship between the *Herald* and one of its readers. As regards the specific circumstances referred to by Lord Devlin, this requires the following to exist — that the party seeking information trusted the other to exercise such a degree of care as the circumstances required, where it was reasonable for him to do that, and where the other gave the information when he knew or ought to have known that the inquirer was relying on him. It is difficult to argue that these conditions existed here. While it is clear that the article was negligently written, the editor could hardly have known that any reader would rely on the advice given. This case can be sharply distinguished from *De La Bere* v *Pearson*, where a newspaper offered individual financial advice from its city editor to the claimant, who had written to the editor asking for the name of a reliable stockbroker. The editor replied suggesting a stockbroker who (unknown to him) was an undischarged bankrupt and who subsequently misappropriated the claimant's money. Here, the editor was held to owe a duty of care because a special relationship existed. In this case, the advice was given generally — not in response to a specific reader's request.

🖉 The candidate gives a full explanation of the general rules governing pure economic loss and the particular rules concerning negligent misstatements, with *Hedley Byrne* being fully explained. There is also a sound application of this rule to the facts, which is considerably strengthened by the distinction drawn between the facts in *De La Bere* and the scenario.

In *Smith* v *Bush*, liability was imposed on surveyors who negligently valued a house because they knew their survey report would be shown to the prospective house buyers and would be relied upon. It was held that the surveyors had 'assumed responsibility' to the house buyers. There would appear no grounds for believing the newspaper had believing any responsibility to Gordon.

question

Finally, in *James McNaughton Paper Groups* v *Hicks Anderson*, where the defendant accountants became aware that the claimants were considering a takeover of their clients, it was held that no duty of care was owed. The draft accounts that they had been asked to confirm in general terms to the claimants had not been prepared for their benefit and the defendant would reasonably expect a party to a takeover bid to take independent advice and not rely exclusively on these draft accounts.

Here, a similar argument could be advanced on behalf of the *Herald* newspaper. The editor could not reasonably expect any reader, far less a professional businessman, to rely exclusively on that article and buy the security software package without taking further steps to ensure Safestore could be installed to protect his clients' confidential business information.

In conclusion, Gordon would appear to have no rights against the *Herald*.

> The reference to these additional cases confirms the candidate's sound grasp of the key rules of economic loss arising from negligent misstatement, and provides the basis of a well-reasoned application and conclusion. Above all, this answer demonstrates how thoroughly candidates need to understand the facts of key cases and then how to use these to provide a strong argument and conclusion.
>
> Overall, this answer deals with all relevant content issues soundly — both in terms of explaining legal rules and applying them — and so would be awarded 24 or 25 marks.

■ ■ ■

C-grade answer

In this scenario between the *Herald* newspaper and Gordon, the newspaper has printed an article in which it recommends a software package. Gordon has read the article and followed the recommendation. As a result, Gordon has suffered considerable economic loss. He has had to pay out £30,000 and is not getting any more orders for his services.

Economic loss is not recoverable in negligence unless it is a consequence of personal injury or damage to property, or is caused by a negligent misstatement. In this case it is possible that Gordon could sue the *Herald* on the basis of a negligent misstatement.

The leading case on negligent misstatement is *Hedley Byrne*. In this case, an advertising company asked a bank for a reference about a client. The bank gave a favourable reference. However, the client then went into liquidation, which caused loss to the advertising company amounting to £17,000. The House of Lords held that there was a duty to give careful advice in certain situations but that in this case the bank was not liable because it had put a disclaimer in the reference. The House of Lords said that a duty of care arose to give careful advice where a special relationship existed between the parties.

While the Law Lords gave differing accounts as to what amounts to a special relationship, there were common elements that emerged from their judgements. First, the person giving the advice must possess special skill in giving that sort of advice. In the scenario, the advice is given in the computer pages, and people writing computer pages would have special skill regarding computer software packages. Furthermore, the advice is not given in a social situation. Second, the person who suffers loss must rely on the advice. In this case we are told that Gordon read the article and then bought the package. We are not told that he sought or received other advice. Therefore, it would seem that Gordon relied on the information in the article. Finally, it must be reasonable for the claimant to rely on the statement. Guidelines were given in *Caparo* v *Dickman* on circumstances where reliance is reasonable. In this scenario, the reliance will probably not be considered reasonable. This is because the people writing the article would not know specifically who would read it. They would also probably expect the people reading the article to get other advice. There is also the point that a lot of people would read the article and if the authors of the article could potentially be liable to all the readers this would extend their liability too far. The law in this area has been developed to limit the liability of the defendant and to prevent the so-called 'opening of the floodgates'.

In conclusion, it is doubtful that the *Herald* will be liable to Gordon for the economic loss he has suffered.

> This answer indicates that the candidate has general knowledge of the law relating to negligent misstatement and is able to apply that knowledge to the specific points raised in the question. There is explanation of the leading case of *Hedley Byrne* and the requirements of a special relationship, which are then applied to the scenario. The guidelines of *Caparo* are mentioned and briefly explored. The candidate could have enhanced the answer with further case law. Notice the lack of case law generally compared to the A-grade answer. The answer is also weakened as there is only a passing mention of negligence and consequently no specific consideration of negligence being the basis of recovery. This is a common omission of weaker candidates. The answer would be awarded 15 or 16 marks.

Occupiers' liability

Gordon engaged Ian to repair damage to a wall in his house. While doing so, Ian cut through an electricity cable and fused the power supply. Gordon was out, so Ian opened the locked door to the cellar with a key hanging from a nail on a nearby wall. As he went down the cellar stairs to find the electricity unit, a rotten stair gave way under his weight and he fell, breaking his leg and ripping his clothes.

Source: January 2004, AQA Paper 5, question 3(b)

Consider what rights Ian may have against Gordon in connection with his broken leg and his ripped clothes.

(25 marks)

■ ■ ■

A-grade answer

The issue of what rights Ian may have against Gordon depends largely on whether Ian was a lawful visitor or a trespasser at the time when he opened the cellar door and fell through the rotten stairs.

The law dealing with an occupier's liability towards lawful visitors is contained in the Occupiers' Liability Act 1957, which codified the common law duty of care. In s.2 this is a duty to take such care as is reasonable in the circumstances to see that the visitor will be reasonably safe in using the premises for the purposes for which he is invited or permitted to be there. Clearly, Ian is a lawful visitor in respect of the repair to Gordon's wall and Gordon is the occupier as it is his house and he has a sufficient degree of control over it, as stipulated by Lord Denning in *Wheat* v *Lacon* (1966).

As Ian is presumably an expert tradesman — probably a builder — the appropriate section to be considered is s.2(3)(b) of the 1957 Act. This states that an occupier who invites tradesmen to enter his/her premises to carry out their ordinary work is entitled to assume that they are aware of any special risks associated with that work and that they will take precautions accordingly. The leading case on this issue is that of *Roles* v *Nathan*, where the Court of Appeal held that the warning given by the occupier to the chimney sweeps had been adequate, given that the sweeps were exercising their profession and should have already been aware of the dangers.

In the case in question, it is at least questionable whether cutting through an electricity cable could be regarded as a special risk associated with the task of repairing a wall. There is no indication in the scenario that Gordon warned Ian about the presence of an electricity cable. If the cable actually ran through the wall in an unusual direction, it could be argued that Gordon breached his common-law duty to Ian by failing to warn him. Furthermore, it is doubtful that a rotten staircase to a basement would be regarded as a risk incidental to plastering a wall. Lord Denning hypothesised on this very scenario in *Roles* v *Nathan* when he stated that the defendants would not have been liable if the stairs leading to the basement had given way, as this was not a risk ordinarily incidental to the work of a chimney sweep. If the risk is not incidental to the work of the expert visitor, the law is clear — the fact that the visitor is an expert will not in itself free the occupier from liability if the expert is injured as a foreseeable consequence of negligence by the occupier. This was the position in *Ogwo* v *Taylor*, decided on the basis of common-law negligence, where the householder who started a fire by his careless use of a blowlamp was liable for injuries suffered by a fireman fighting the fire.

Having fused the power supply in the absence of Gordon, it would be foreseeable that a tradesman would try to carry out the relatively straightforward task of replacing the fuse by locating the fuse box. There was no notice warning anyone not to enter the cellar — indeed the proximity of the key (which was hanging from a nail on a nearby wall) strengthens Ian's case to be a lawful visitor. On the simple principle of the 'neighbour test' in *Donoghue* v *Stevenson*, in these circumstances it would not be difficult to establish that Gordon owed Ian a duty of care, which he breached and which was the cause of Ian's injury and his ripped clothes. Ian would therefore be able to claim damages for both the injury and the cost of replacing his ripped clothes.

> ℮ This response begins effectively. The answer immediately addresses the key issue of this question — is Ian a lawful visitor or a trespasser? The answer continues by dealing with the rules in the 1957 Act in detail, particularly the issue of Ian being 'an expert tradesman', so invoking s.2(3)(b). The candidate makes good use of case authorities, and the reference to *Donoghue* is helpful in dealing with the duty of care question. There is sensible speculation as to the foreseeability of Ian's actions.

However, it is necessary to consider the alternative position — that Ian, although initially a lawful visitor, became a trespasser as soon as he entered the cellar. If the visitor ceases to use the premises for the purpose for which he/she is invited to be there, then no duty is owed under the 1957 Act. As Scrutton LJ stated in *The Calgarth* (1927): 'When you invite a person into your house to use the stairs, you do not invite him to slide down the banisters.' Prior to the case of *Herrington* v *British Rail Board*, the law was severe — no duty of care was owed to trespassers. The decision in that case was incorporated in the Occupiers' Liability Act 1984, which by s.1(3) imposed a duty to trespassers in the following circumstances:

(i) The occupier is aware of the danger or has reasonable grounds to believe that it exists.

(ii) The occupier knows or has reasonable grounds to believe that the trespasser is in the vicinity of the danger or that he may come into the vicinity of the danger.

(iii) The risk is one against which, in all the circumstances of the case, the occupier may reasonably be expected to offer the other some protection.

Here, it could be argued that Gordon was aware of the rotten state of the cellar stair — if the main electricity supply of his house came into his cellar, he would surely have

entered the cellar occasionally to check the meter reading, if for no other reason. The second test could also be met — the fact that the key to the cellar was 'hanging from a nail on a nearby wall' is certainly suggestive of the likelihood of someone entering the cellar. The final requirement — that the risk is one against which Gordon may be expected to offer Ian some protection — is surely also satisfied. At the very least, the key should not have been so readily available or Gordon should have placed a warning notice on the door or given Ian a specific warning against entering the cellar.

However, although it can be argued that Gordon was liable under s.1(8) of the 1984 Act for Ian's broken leg, he would not be liable for the damage to Ian's clothing — this section specifically provides that trespassers are not entitled to sue in respect of property damage.

> There is a sound explanation *and* application of all three basic rules under s.1(3) of the 1984 Act, and the final issue under s.1(8) is correctly covered. Too often candidates only list the rules without attempting to consider their application in the specific circumstances of the scenario, but they can only be adequately explained in context. The answer also deals soundly with both the lawful visitor and the trespasser. It would receive the full 25 marks.

■ ■ ■

C-grade answer

It is possible that Ian may have rights against Gordon under the Occupiers' Liability Acts 1957 and 1984. The 1957 Act deals with visitors and the 1984 Act deals with non-visitors. In this scenario it is likely that both of these Acts will be of relevance.

In respect of an action under either Act, it will be necessary for Ian to show that Gordon is the occupier. Both Acts impose a duty on anyone who has a sufficient degree of control over the premises. Both Acts refer to the common law on this issue. The leading case is *Wheat* v *Lacon*. A guest at a public house fell down the stairs and was killed. Lord Denning said: 'Wherever a person has a sufficient degree of control over premises...then he is an occupier.' It is possible for there to be more than one occupier. In this case it was held that the manager, who occupied the premises as an employee, and the owners were all occupiers. In the question, it is clear that Gordon is the occupier.

Under the 1957 Act a duty is owed to visitors. Section 1(2) states that a duty is owed to those people who under common law would have been invitees and licensees. An invitee was someone who entered the premises with permission of the occupier on business of interests to him or herself and the occupier. A licensee was someone who with the occupier's permission entered the premises for his/her own purposes. Under s.5(1) a duty is also owed to people who have a contractual right to enter the premises. It would appear that Ian is a visitor.

Under the 1957 Act, the visitor can claim for personal injury and damage to property, including property belonging to another. This is stated in s.1(3)(b).

The duty owed to Ian by Gordon is the common-law duty of care, stated in s.2(2) as 'a duty to take such care as in all the circumstances of the case is reasonable to see that the visitor will be reasonably safe in using the premises for the purposes for which he is invited or permitted by the occupier to be there'.

Under the 1957 Act, a greater duty is owed to children and a lesser duty is owed to experts. Section 2(3)(b) states that the occupier may expect the expert visitor to guard against risks ordinarily incidental to his/her work. In *Roles* v *Nathan*, two chimney sweeps died when they were overcome by fumes while cleaning flues. The chimney sweeps should have guarded against the risk of this as it was incidental to their work. It is important to emphasise that only the risks incidental to the expert are to be guarded against by the visitor. Lord Denning in this case said the position would have been different if the sweeps had been killed as a result of a staircase to the basement giving way. As Ian is a plasterer, he would be expected to be aware of risks to do with plastering.

It is possible that Ian may also be a trespasser and so be covered under the 1984 Act. As Scrutton LJ stated in *The Calgarth* (1927): 'When you invite someone into your house to use the stairs, you do not invite them to slide down the banisters.'

The 1984 Act is concerned with people who are classed as non-visitors. Occupiers are the same people as under the 1957 Act and as the term 'non-visitors' implies, these are people who do not fall within the classification of visitors under the 1957 Act. It is possible that Ian could also be a non-visitor.

A duty is owed under the 1984 Act in three circumstances stipulated in s.1(3). First, the occupier must be aware of the danger or have reasonable grounds to believe that it exists. Second, the occupier must know, or have reasonable grounds to believe, that the trespasser is in the vicinity of the danger or may come into the vicinity. Third, the risk must be one against which in all the circumstances of the case the occupier may reasonably be expected to offer the trespasser some protection. If the circumstances in the scenario between Ian and Gordon satisfy these criteria then the duty owed is stated in s.1(4) as being to take such care as in all the circumstances is reasonable to see that the non-visitor does not suffer injury by reason of the danger concerned.

The 1984 Act does not allow for compensation to be paid in respect of damage to property, so under this Act Ian would not get any money for the damage to his clothing.

✎ This answer covers the law relevant to the question well. However, there is little application. Candidates should note from the mark scheme that answers containing no application can never be awarded more than 15 marks, however thorough the explanation of the law may be. There is a little application here regarding the difference between the Acts as to damage to property being recoverable, and an inadequate attempt at application is made in respect of the law on experts. This answer would be awarded 17 marks.

Nuisance and *Rylands* v *Fletcher*

Residents living in the vicinity of the Johnsons factory had been complaining for some time of the noise and vibration coming from the factory, especially at night. When an explosion occurred in the factory one morning, a thick cloud of smoke spread rapidly across the town, leaving a dirty, oily deposit on houses and other buildings.

Source: January 2004, AQA Paper 5, Question 4(a)

Consider what rights and indicate what remedies residents of the houses affected by the noise, vibration and explosion may have against Johnsons. (25 marks)

■ ■ ■

A-grade answer

The tort of private nuisance is concerned with the protection of interests in land, and the restrictions imposed on an occupier in order that an occupier of adjacent land is not unreasonably disturbed. It is ill defined, but it is best described as a substantial and unreasonable interference with the claimant's land or with his/her enjoyment of it. There are different types of damage that can amount to a private nuisance: physical damage to the claimant's property, loss of value to the claimant's property (though this is uncertain), and interference with the claimant's enjoyment of his/her property. Examples include excessive noise or causing dust or noxious smells.

In the case of *Christie* v *Davey*, the claimant and the defendant lived in adjoining houses. The claimant was a music teacher who gave lessons at home and sometimes held musical parties. The defendant objected to this and retaliated by blowing whistles, banging on metal trays, shouting and making noise to disturb the music. The claimant was granted an injunction.

The party who can bring action in private nuisance must normally be a person with a legal or equitable interest in the land affected by the nuisance; a mere relative or visitor has no cause for action. This principle was seen in the case of *Malone* v *Laskey* and affirmed in 1997 by the House of Lords in *Hunter* v *Canary Wharf*.

The whole law of private nuisance is a matter of balancing competing interests — the occupier's right to use his/her land as he/she wishes, against the neighbour's right to enjoy his/her land — and depends very much on questions of reasonableness. With regards to duration of the nuisance, it is a general rule that the courts will not grant relief against a nuisance unless the interference is of substantial duration.

> *e* This is a straightforward introductory section in which the rules of private nuisance are clearly explained, with good use being made of supporting cases.

With reference to the scenario, it is obvious that the people complaining are the occupiers of the houses or those who would have a legal interest in the houses, and so they would have an automatic right to claim against Johnsons. Johnsons would most likely be held liable instead of the owner of the factory or the person running it and Johnsons would be held accountable for the actions as Johnsons would have control over operating times. It can be argued from the scenario that the nuisance must have been occurring for a substantial time, as the residents have been complaining for 'some time'. Therefore, this may mean that the courts could grant relief against the nuisance. The remedies that may be available to the residents would include damages or an injunction to restrain the continuation of the nuisance. An injunction is usually the preferred remedy for the claimant, as it requires the defendant to bring the nuisance to an end. It also has the advantage of flexibility, as it can be tailored to meet the exact circumstances of the case and produce a just solution. In this case, the residents may be awarded damages but the most likely result would be to give an injunction. This could mean that Johnsons could only operate during certain hours and have to stop at a certain time at night. Another remedy, which would be most favoured by Johnsons, is for the court to order Johnsons to install better sound insulation which would enable them to operate during the night without causing as much inconvenience to the residents.

> 🖉 Having laid out the relevant rules, these are now applied with reference to the scenario. The issue of remedies is also addressed (this is a frequent omission).

The noise, vibration and explosion produced by the factory could also be classed as a public nuisance, especially the explosion. A public nuisance (which is a crime as well as a tort) is an act or omission not warranted by law that affects the comfort and convenience of a whole group of people. The harm does not just have to be something that affects the land; it can be damage to goods or financial loss. The facts in this case are similar to the case of *Attorney General* v *PYA Quarries*. In this case, residents living near a quarry were disturbed by vibrations from the explosion and by the dust that spread throughout the district in dry weather. At the request of local authorities, the Attorney General sought and was granted an injunction restraining the quarry owners from conducting their work in such a manner as to occasion nuisance to Her Majesty's subjects by dust or by vibration.

> 🖉 Where a number of people have been affected by a particular nuisance, candidates should be prepared to consider public nuisance as well as private, although, as illustrated above, this topic can be covered quickly. All the key points are dealt with — definition, leading case and injunctive remedy. Although the application of these rules to the facts is lacking, some credit may be transferred from the previous part of the answer.

The tort of *Rylands* v *Fletcher* has its origins in the law of nuisance but has developed as a separate tort with its own rules. The tort imposes liability for the escape of something from land, which then causes damage. The tort was defined by Blackburn J: in his judgement in *R* v *F* he said that a person who, for his own purposes, brings on his

land and collects and keeps there anything likely to do mischief if it escapes, must keep it at his peril and, if he does not do so, then he is answerable for all the damage that is the natural consequence of the escape. Lord Cairns in the House of Lords drew a distinction between what he described as 'natural use', such as the natural accumulation of rain water, and 'non-natural use', such as the storage of water in a purpose-built reservoir. In the case of a natural use, there would be no liability for damage caused by escape. In the case of *Rylands* v *Fletcher*, the defendant had employed an independent contractor to build a reservoir on his land. Due to the contractor's negligence, water escaped through some old mine workings and flooded current workings on the claimant's land a short distance away. It was held that the claimant was entitled to damages on the basis of what has become known as the tort of *R* v *F*.

With regards to dangerous things, the definition states that the thing accumulated must be dangerous in itself, and that it must be likely to cause damage if it escapes. The defendant is liable for the damage caused by an escape. This basically requires the thing to move from the defendant's land to cause damage elsewhere. If there is no escape then there can be no liability. There is some flexibility, in as much as a fire or the blast of an explosion should probably be treated as a 'dangerous substance'. The case of *Read* v *Lyons* can be distinguished from the case of Johnsons. While both cases involved an explosion, in *Read* v *Lyons* the claimant was injured and the claim failed as no escape occurred. Lord Bingham, in the case of *Transco* v *Stockport MBC*, said that it had been suggested by some that the rule in *R* v *F* should be abolished and appropriate cases be dealt with through ordinary negligence. The rule in *R* v *F* applies to only 'non-natural' use of the land, and only where the thing that escapes is likely to cause danger. With reference to the scenario, the factory was not a natural use of the land and as a result there was an escape of dust, leaving dirty, oily deposits on houses and other buildings. It is clear that this dust would satisfy the definition of being a dangerous thing, as it was likely to and did indeed cause damage. Johnsons would therefore be liable for the dirt on the buildings and houses, as it was caused by an escape.

As for the remedies that may be available with reference to the explosion, general damages would be most suitable. An injunction would not be appropriate, as it is not a regular occurrence. Any damages awarded would be compensatory for the damage done to the houses and buildings.

> 🖉 Note how this part of the answer is structured — the first section explains all the legal rules in *Rylands* v *Fletcher*, whereas the second section covers the application. The separate issue of remedies is dealt with effectively. This answer would receive 24 or 25 marks.

■ ■ ■

C-grade answer

The residents would probably be able to bring an action in nuisance. There are two types of nuisance — private and public. Private nuisance actions can be brought by the individuals who are affected by the nuisance. Public nuisance actions are brought by the Attorney General on behalf of the people affected. To be a public nuisance, the activity must affect a class of the public. This is what was said in the *PYA Quarries* case.

In the situation with the Johnsons factory, the residents would be able to sue, as long as they have a legal interest in the land affected. This was established in *Malone* v *Laskey*. It would appear that there is a nuisance being caused by the Johnsons factory because the question says there is noise and vibration coming from it. The question also says that the residents have been complaining for some time, which means that the noise and vibrations have been causing the residents a problem for some time and not just once or twice. In *Miller* v *Jackson*, balls were hit into the claimant's garden on several occasions. Also in the Johnsons case, there has been a thick cloud of smoke that has left an oily deposit on the houses and other buildings. This is like the case in which plants were damaged and, even though the area was semi-industrial, this was still a nuisance.

It is possible that the nuisance in this case could be a public nuisance. This is because there are a number of residents being affected by the noise and vibrations.

In a nuisance action, the claimant usually wants to stop the nuisance. This means the remedy they want is an injunction. In this scenario, the residents would want an injunction because they want the noise and vibrations to stop. An injunction is an order of the court. It is possible that the courts might order the factory to only work at certain times or to change the way it works so that there is less noise and vibration.

The rule in *Rylands* v *Fletcher* may be relevant. There has been an explosion and oily deposits have been left on some of the houses and buildings. This means that there has been an escape of the oil from the factory. For an action under the rule to succeed, the factory would need to be a non-natural use of land, which it probably would be because factories are not naturally on land. Therefore, the residents might be able to claim compensation for the damage caused to their houses.

> ✐ This answer would be awarded 16 or 17 marks. The key legal issues relevant to the question are all mentioned. However, compared with the A-grade answer there is little authority or development. Note that the remedy of damages is merely identified and the material relating to *Rylands* v *Fletcher* is extremely brief.

Evaluation of economic loss

Consider whether the law relating to recovery of compensation for economic loss is in need of reform. (25 marks)

■ ■ ■

A-grade answer

The law regarding the duty of care owed in respect of economic loss has been developed piecemeal by the judiciary. There is no statutory provision. It follows that there has therefore been no comprehensive research conducted into this area of law with a view to its codification. Consequently, the law in this area is unpredictable and uncertain in the scope of its application.

The law on economic loss has largely been developed with policy considerations in mind. Two policies often referred to by judges are the need to limit the number of cases being brought before the courts (the 'floodgates policy'), and the desire to limit the liability of the defendant to a sensible level. As Cardozo CJ said in *Ultramares Corporation* v *Touche* (1931), the defendant would otherwise be subjected to 'liability in an indeterminate amount for an indeterminate time to an indeterminate class'.

Basing development of the law on economic loss on policy has had the effect of creating an artificial distinction between what is considered to be pure economic loss and what is considered to be consequential economic loss. In *Weller* v *The Foot and Mouth Disease Research Institute* (1965), the auctioneer was unable to recover compensation for his loss of profit suffered as a result of the restriction of movement of cattle. There had been no damage to his premises or personal injury to himself, so his loss was purely economic. The same principle can be seen in *Spartan Steel and Alloys Ltd* v *Martin and Co (Contractors) Ltd* (1972). The claimant could recover for the loss of profit that would have been made on the melt being processed at the time of the power-cut, as that was consequential on physical damage to property. However, no compensation could be recovered for the loss of profit that the claimant would have made on melts planned to be processed later that same day.

The decision in *Spartan Steel* was justified by Lord Denning on policy grounds. He said that there was a need to restrict the potential number of fake/fictitious or exaggerated claims that may otherwise be brought, were the distinction between pure and consequential economic loss not made.

This distinction between pure and consequential loss is nevertheless a fine one, and in terms of foreseeability and causation, the key concepts of a negligence action, it is difficult to justify. In *Spartan Steel*, the defendants' negligence caused all three types of loss to be suffered, i.e. the physical damage to the melt, the consequential loss of profit on the damaged melt, and the loss of profit the claimant sustained as a result of not being able to process any further melts that day. Furthermore, all these three types of loss were foreseeable. However, compensation could only be recovered in respect of the first two types.

There is no doubt that the law preventing recovery of compensation for pure economic loss has limited the liability of the defendant. However, it can be argued that the position now is that the defendant gets off lightly, paying only a small amount of compensation for the all too often huge amount of loss they have caused. This can clearly be seen to be the case in both *Spartan Steel* and *Weller* v *The Foot and Mouth Disease Research Institute.*

While no compensation may be recovered in respect of pure economic loss caused by negligent acts, the claimant may nevertheless make a claim in respect of economic loss caused by a negligent misstatement. The House of Lords (*in obiter*), in *Hedley Byrne and Co Ltd* v *Heller and Partners Ltd* (1964), approved the dissenting judgement of Lord Denning in *Candler* v *Crane Christmas and Co* (1951), and held that a duty of care arose in respect of negligently made statements causing economic loss, provided that a special relationship exists between the parties. Subsequent decisions have highlighted the inadequacy of the special relationship requirements.

One problematic issue concerning the scope of the special relationship is the unclear position regarding social and domestic situations following the decision of *Chaudry* v *Prabhakar* (1988). It is clear that people should be able to make claims for losses which arise during the course of business, but social situations should not give rise to such actions. Enabling family members and friends to sue one another seems to be in contrast to the policy decisions made to restrict the number of cases brought before the courts. However, people should be encouraged to seek professional advice and, if through the negligence of such professionals people suffer loss, then of course they should have legal redress. This seems logical and is the reason for companies having insurance.

The cases of *White* v *Jones* (1995) and *Spring* v *Guardian Assurance plc* (1994) arguably demonstrate that the special relationship criteria are inadequate in providing justice in all deserving cases where loss is suffered as a result of a negligent misstatement. In neither case could the claimants be said to have acted in reliance to their detriment as a result of what the defendants had stated.

One particular area in which the law on economic loss has raised issues is that concerning the negligent inspection of building foundations and the subsequent depletion of value in a property. The economic loss suffered by the owners cannot be recovered from those who negligently state that the foundations are adequate, following the decision in *Murphy* v *Brentwood* (1990). Such loss is purely economic, as the building is merely defective. The foundations are not to be treated as separate to the building they support, so the foundations cannot be said to have caused damage to property, the building as a whole has only damaged itself. This decision clearly has harsh consequences for claimants who suffer such loss and is recognised by the

question

judiciary that had previously held in *Anns* v *Merton London Borough Council* (1978) that loss in these circumstances was recoverable.

A further criticism that becomes evident from the foundations cases is the fact that in some circumstances it is not easy to see whether the claim is being made in respect of a negligent act or a negligent misstatement. If the building inspections, which are usually presented in a report, were treated as statements, then the loss suffered by the claimants in the foundations cases would be recoverable.

Liability for defective products, as repeatedly emphasised by the judiciary, is a matter for contract law. The person who suffers loss as a result of a defective product may, therefore, recover that loss in contract, provided that he/she is in a contractual relationship. The loss is not recoverable in negligence because it is pure economic loss and not consequential upon physical damage to property or personal injury. The case of *Junior Books Ltd* v *Veitchi Co Ltd* (1982), now confined to facts but not overruled, highlights the difficulty faced by judges when dealing with such claims. The Law Lords justified their decision partly on the basis that the relationship between the claimant and defendant was, in the words of Lord Roskill, 'as close as it could be short of actual privity of contract'. The claim in respect of a defective factory floor, laid by the defendant sub-contractors who had been nominated by the claimant, was successful. The loss suffered by the claimant was the cost of repairing the floor and the loss of profit caused by the disruption to the factory, and was therefore purely economic.

In conclusion, it can be seen that there are many areas of the law on economic loss that would benefit from reform. Comprehensive research of this area of law could lead to more satisfactory rules being laid down in the form of a statute. Until the legislature decides to intervene, the judges will have to continue to develop the law in a piecemeal fashion. Furthermore, while the judiciary should not concern itself with policy issues, it is undoubtedly necessary to impose limitations on the scope of the duty of care in this area.

> This is a comprehensive answer, which addresses both the problems with the law relating to economic loss and the justification for the law developing in the way that is has. Arguments are soundly supported by case authority. The answer would be awarded 23 or 24 marks.